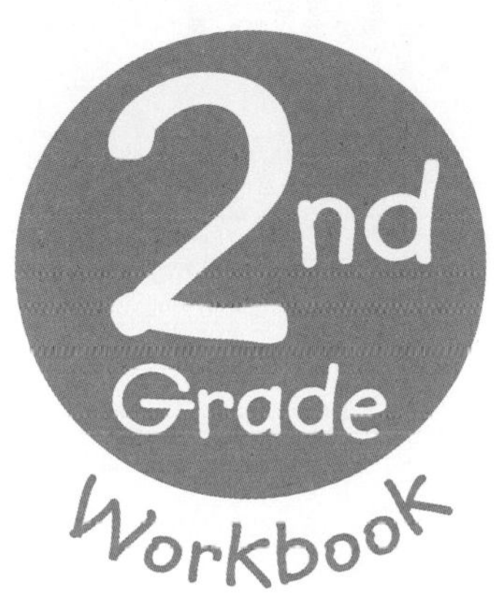

Math

Author Deborah Lock
Consultant Alison Tribley

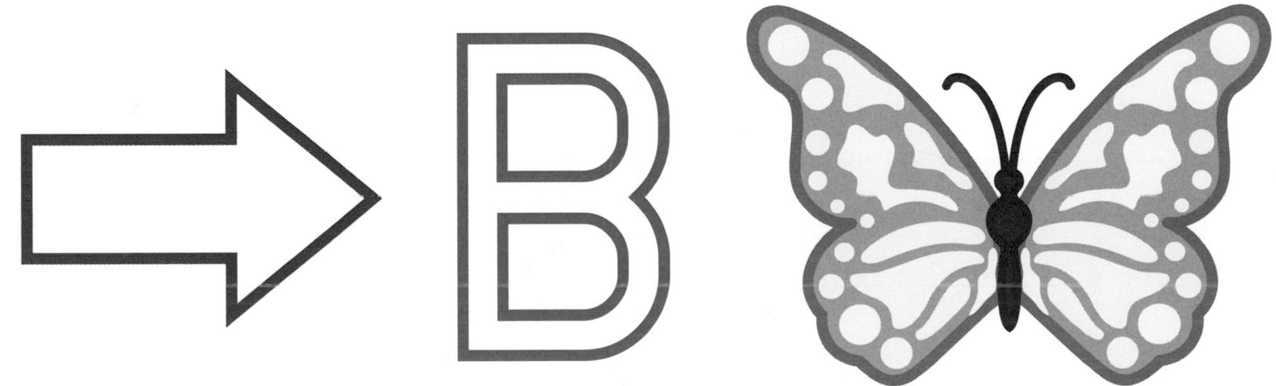

10-minute challenge

Try to complete the exercises for each topic in 10 minutes or less. Note the time it takes you in the "Time taken" column below.

DK London
Editor Elizabeth Blakemore
Senior Editor Deborah Lock
US Editor Nancy Ellwood
Math Consultants Sean McArdle, Alison Tribley
Managing Editor Christine Stroyan
Managing Art Editor Anna Hall
Senior Production Editor Andy Hilliard
Senior Production Controller Jude Crozier
Jacket Design Development Manager Sophia MTT
Publisher Andrew Macintyre
Associate Publishing Director Liz Wheeler
Art Director Karen Self
Publishing Director Jonathan Metcalf

DK Delhi
Senior Editor Rupa Rao
Senior Art Editor Stuti Tiwari Bhatia
Editor Dipika Dasgupta
Art Editors Priyabrata Roy Chowdhury, Anuj Sharma, Aanchal Singal, Priyanka Singh
Managing Editors Soma B. Chowdhury, Kingshuk Ghoshal
Managing Art Editor Govind Mittal
Senior DTP Designer Tarun Sharma
DTP Designers Anita Yadav, Rakesh Kumar, Harish Aggarwal
Senior Jacket Designer Suhita Dharamjit
Jackets Editorial Coordinator Priyanka Sharma

This American Edition, 2020
First American Edition, 2013
Published in the United States by DK Publishing
1745 Broadway, 20th Floor, New York, NY 10019

23 24 10 9 8 7 6 5
005–322717–May/2020

A catalog record for this book is available from the Library of Congress.
ISBN 978-0-7440-3138-6

DK books are available at special discounts when purchased in bulk for sales promotions, premiums, fund-raising, or educational use.
For details, contact: DK Publishing Special Markets, 1745 Broadway, 20th Floor, New York, NY 10019
SpecialSales@dk.com

Printed and bound in China

www.dk.com

This book was made with Forest Stewardship Council™ certified paper - one small step in DK's commitment to a sustainable future.
For more information go to www.dk.com/our-green-pledge

Contents

Time Taken

Time Filler:
In these boxes are some extra challenges to extend your skills. You can do them if you have some time left after finishing the questions. Or these can be stand-alone activities that you can do in 10 minutes.

Place Value

The position of the digits 0–9 in a number gives its value.

1. Write 26 in words.

....

2. What number is this?

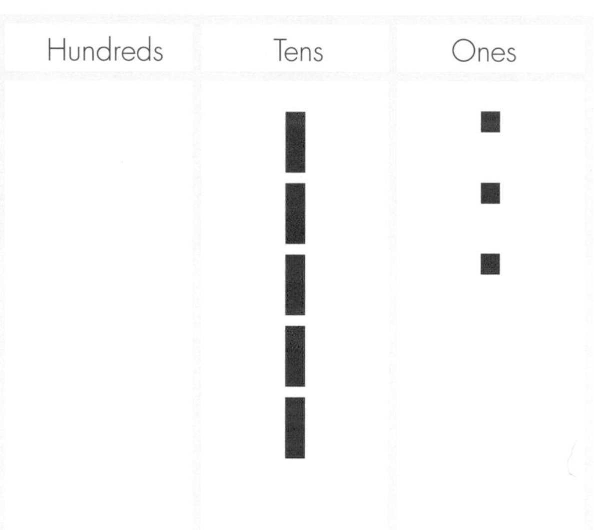

3. Write these numbers as digits.

Twelve	Forty-nine	Seventy-two

4. What is the largest number you can make with the digits 3, 5, and 8?

Time Filler:
Go on a number hunt around the house for 10 minutes. What is the biggest number you can find?

5. Draw the pictures for these numbers. Use these blocks.

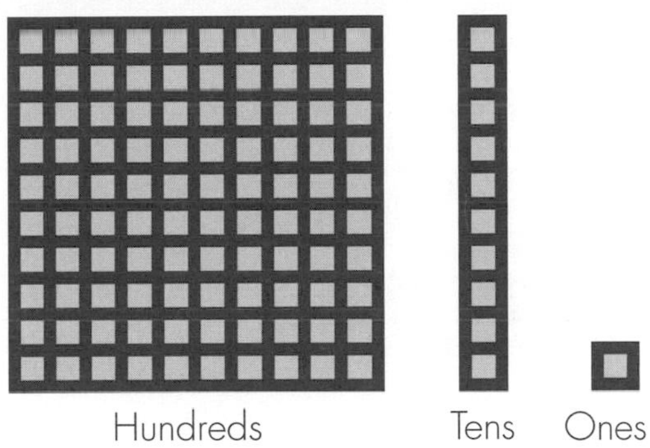

9

37

254

Measuring Length

These questions are all about length.
You will need a ruler.

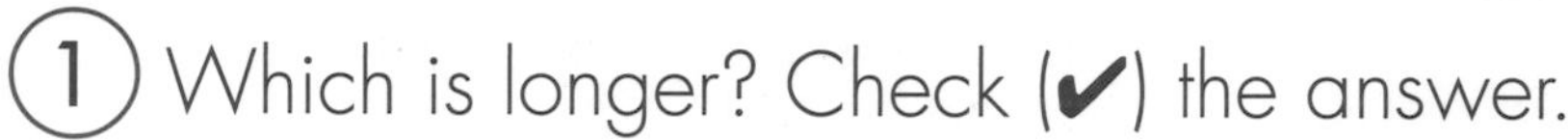

1) Which is longer? Check (✔) the answer.

- [ ] A car
- [ ] A bus

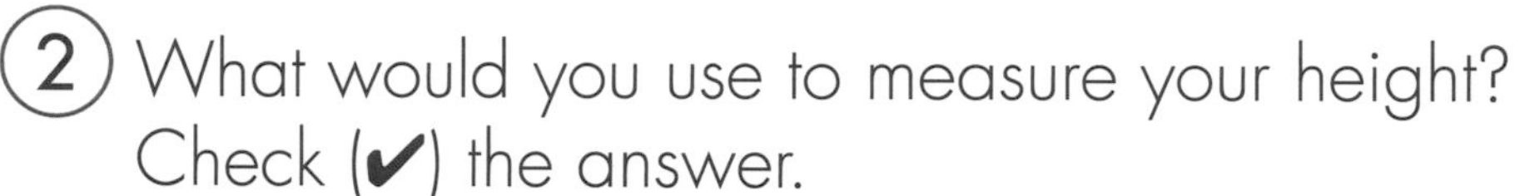

2) What would you use to measure your height?
Check (✔) the answer.

- [ ] Measuring tape
- [ ] Bathroom scales

3) Match the object with its length. Draw a line.

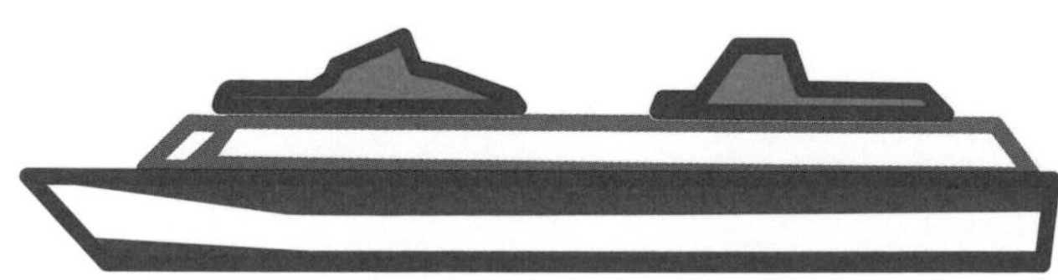

2 meters

345 meters

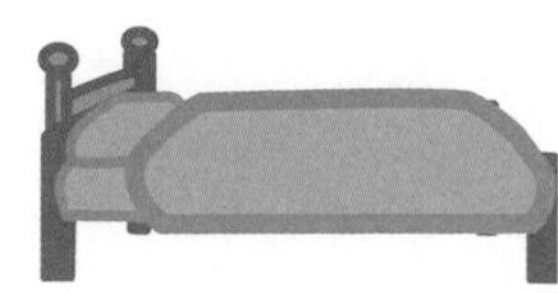

20 centimeters

Time Filler:
Remember: 1 cm = 10 mm, 1 m =100 cm, and 1 km = 1,000 m. Try changing 5 cm into mm (millimeters), 5 m into cm (centimeters), and 5 km into m (meters). Write your own conversion problems like this.

4) How long are these lines in centimeters (cm)? Use a ruler.

5) Jake walked 2 miles to the shop and then walked 2 miles back the same way. How far had he walked altogether?

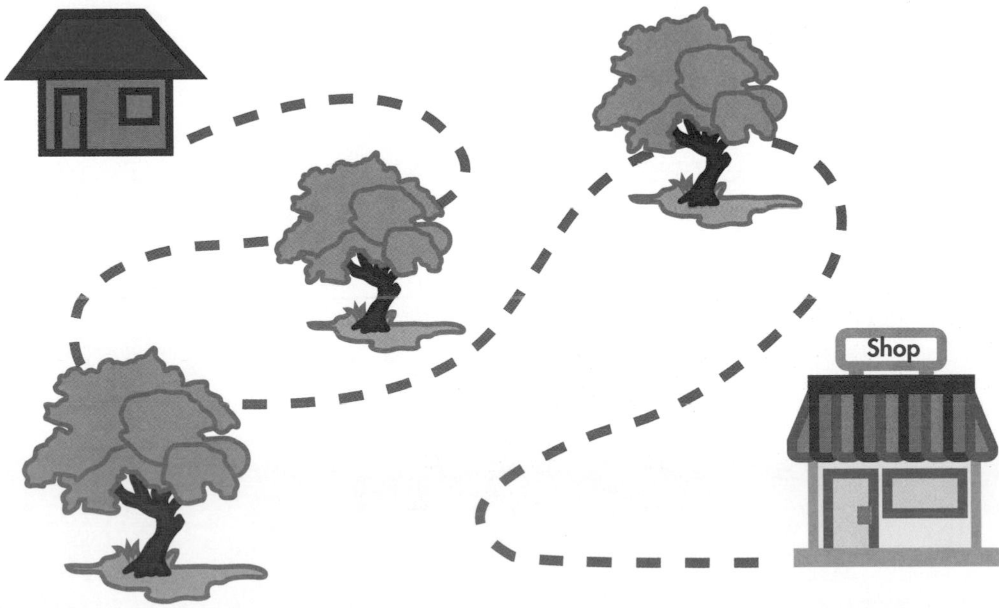

Counting

You will need a die for question 4.

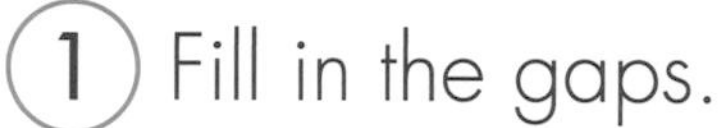

1 Fill in the gaps.

11 12 13  17  19 

2 Which tree has more apples? Check (✔) the answer.

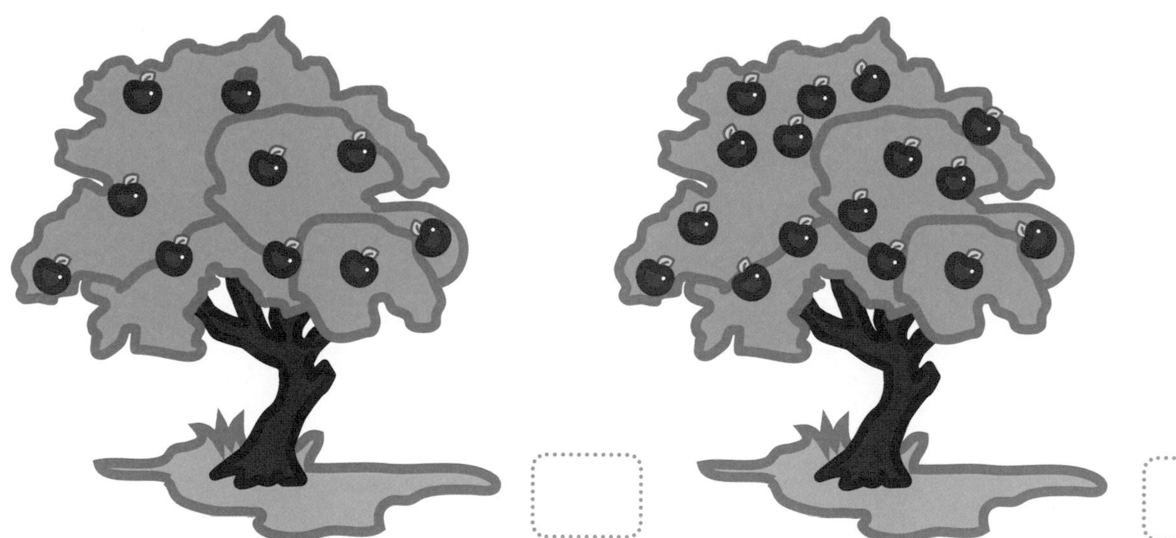

3 How many cookies are on the baking tray?

Time Filler:
Count how many t-shirts you have in your dresser. Count how many plates are in the cupboard and how many mugs are in the kitchen.

(4) Use a die. Start at 0. Roll the die and count on the number shown on the die. Keep rolling the die until you reach the end of the line. Circle the numbers you land on.

0	1	2	3	4	5	6	7	8	9	10	11
											12
24	23	22	21	20	19	18	17	16	15	14	13
25											
26	27	28	29	30	31	32	33	34	35	36	37
											38
50	49	48	47	46	45	44	43	42	41	40	39

(5) Riley put 6 red pens into a jar and then put 7 blue pens in the same jar. How many pens are there in the jar? Use the number line to help you count.

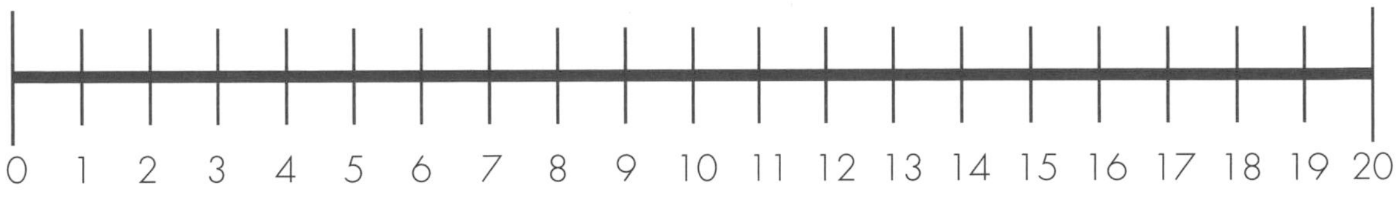

2-D Shapes

A two-dimensional shape is a flat shape. Are you ready to test your knowledge? You will need a ruler.

1) Which shape is a circle? Check (✔) the answer.

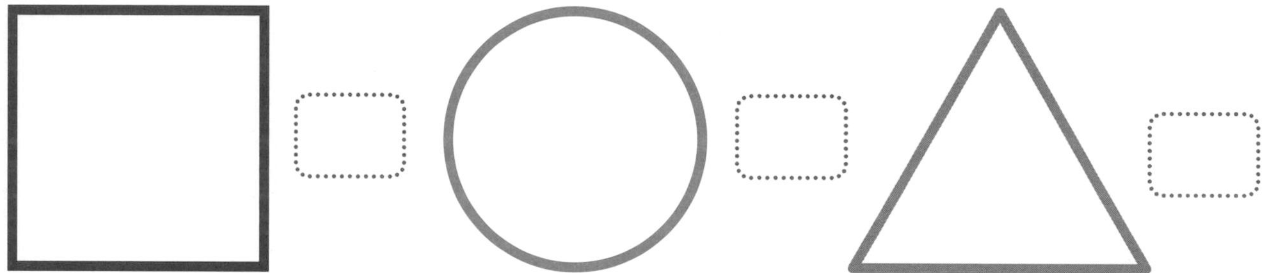

2) How many sides does a rectangle have?

3) Match the shape to its name. Draw a line.

Octagon

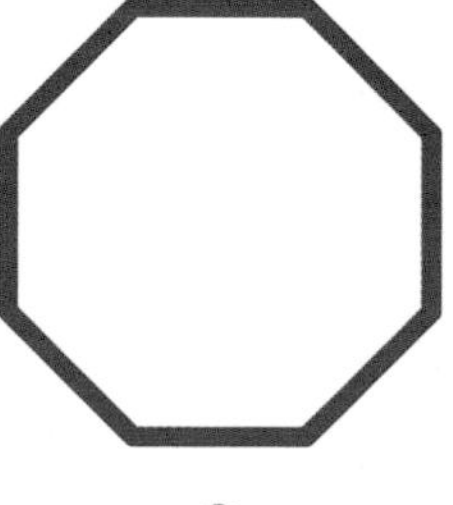

Hexagon

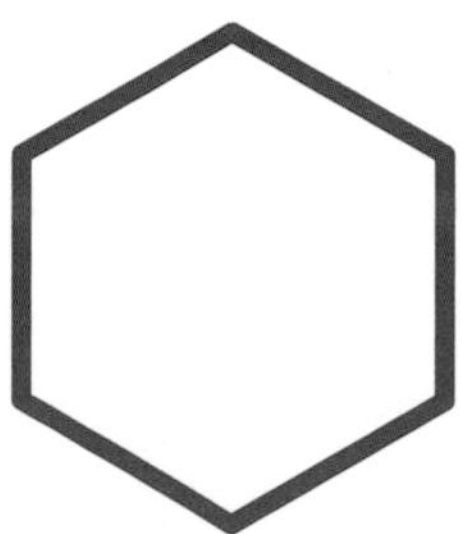

Square

Time Filler:
Remember: A regular shape has all sides and angles that are equal. Can you find any regular shapes in your home? Are the windows regular? Is it easier to find regular or irregular shapes?

4) Which shape is regular? Check (✔) the answer.

5) Use a ruler. Draw a triangle.

Counting in Leaps

Try counting in 2s, 5s, and 10s. Get set, go!

1. Count in 2s. Fill in the gaps.

2 ☐ 6 ☐ 10 ☐ ☐ 16 ☐ 20

2. Here is a number line. Start at 7 and show the leaps to add 2 more each time.

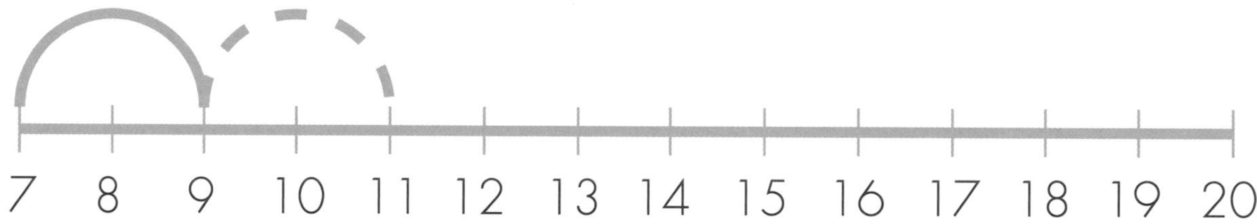

3. Fill in the missing numbers.

12 22 32 ☐ ☐ 62 ☐

5 10 ☐ 20 ☐ ☐ 35 ☐

24 22 ☐ 18 ☐ 14 ☐ 10

Time Filler:
Can you count backward from 100 in 10s? Now try counting backward from 200 in 10s.

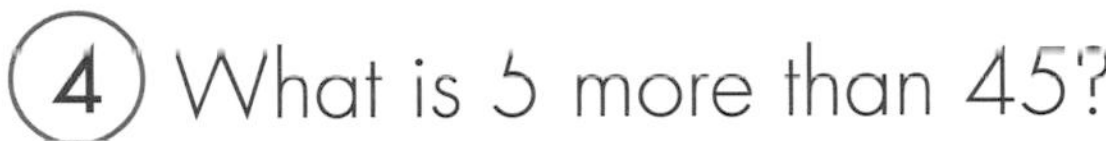

(4) What is 5 more than 45?

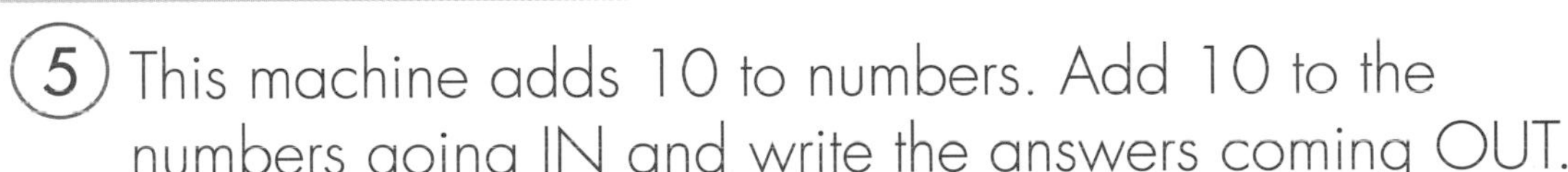

(5) This machine adds 10 to numbers. Add 10 to the numbers going IN and write the answers coming OUT.

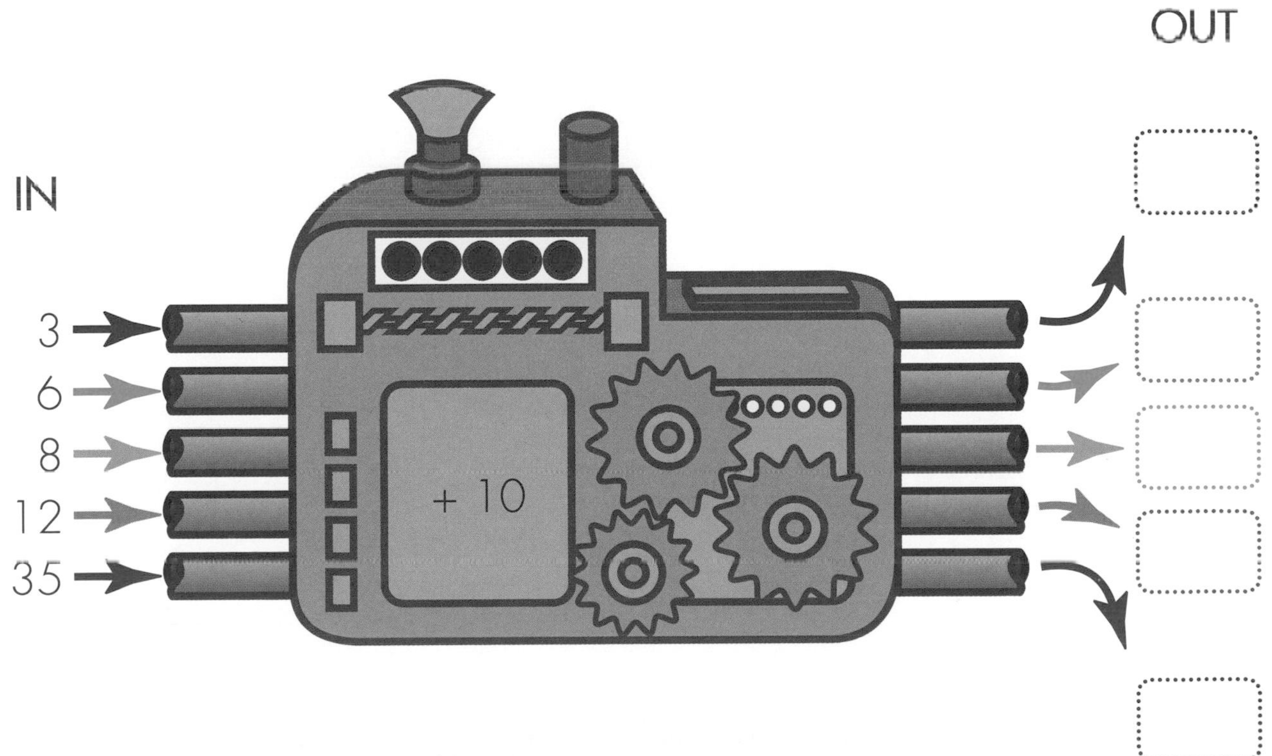

Tables and Charts

Showing information on tables and charts is a useful way of reading and comparing that information. Give it a try!

Twenty children in a class were asked to vote for their favorite wild animals. The results were shown on this table.

Wild Animal	Number of Children
Elephant	4
Lion	5
Monkey	3
Hippo	2
Tiger	4
Giraffe	2

(1) Which was the most popular wild animal?

....

(2) How many children voted for the monkey?

[ ]

(3) Which animals had the least votes?

....

Time Filler:
Ask your family and friends to vote for their favorite wild animal. Choose either a table or chart to show the number of votes for each animal.

(4) Look at the table and color the correct number of squares on the chart below.

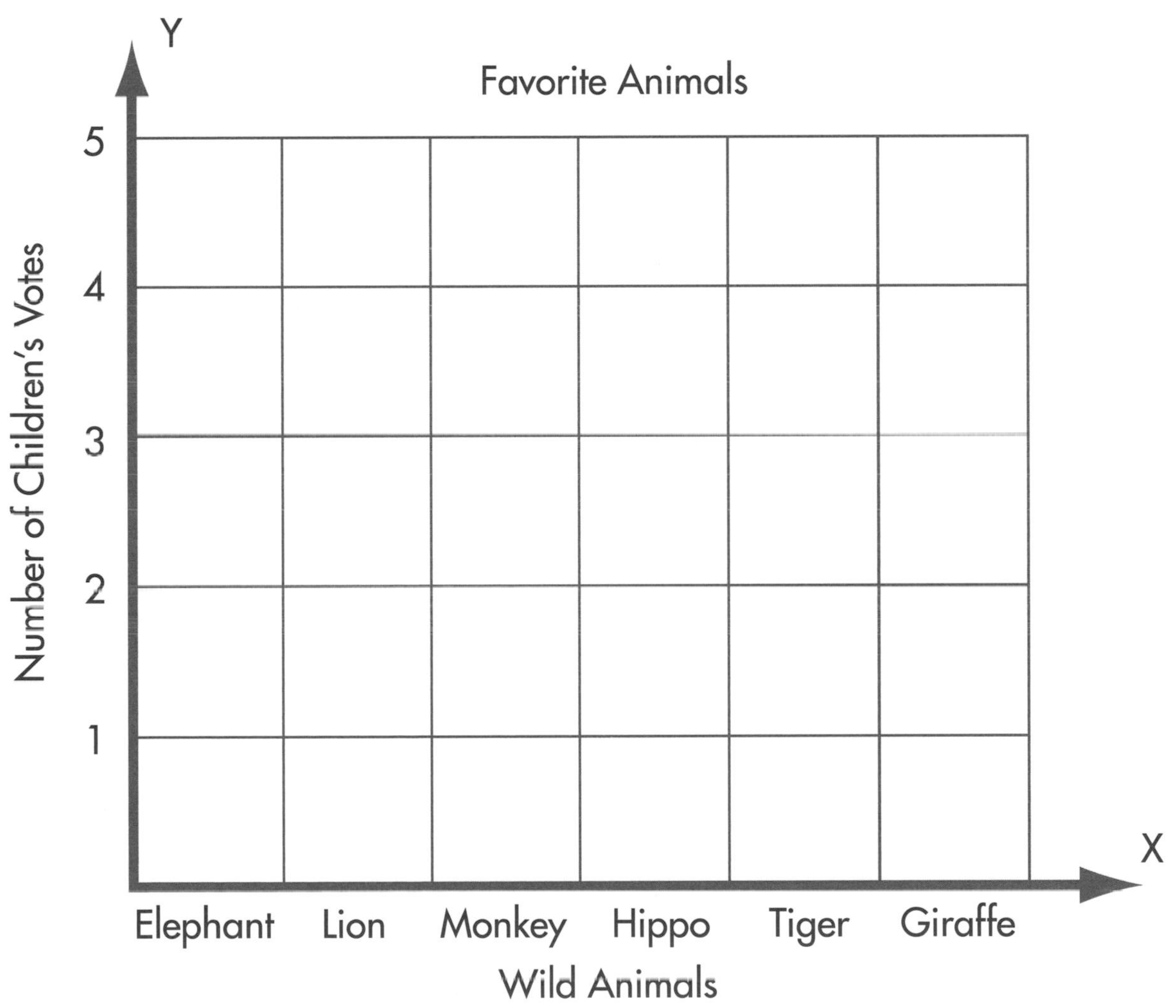

(5) Looking at the chart, how many more children voted for the elephant than the hippo?

Number Order

Here is some number fun!
Put the numbers in the correct order.

1. Put these numbers in the correct order. Start from the smallest.

36 75 24 9 52

☐ ☐ ☐ ☐ ☐

2. What comes next?

56 57 58 ☐ ☐ ☐

27 32 37 ☐ ☐ ☐

63 66 69 ☐ ☐ ☐

3. Circle the largest number.

26 19 37 31

Time Filler:
How many numbers can you make using one or more of the digits 4, 8, and 2? Write them down and then write them again in order. Start with the smallest number.

4) Put these numbers in the correct order. Start from the biggest.

67 42 53 48 59

5) Which number is halfway between 16 and 24?
Use the number line to help.

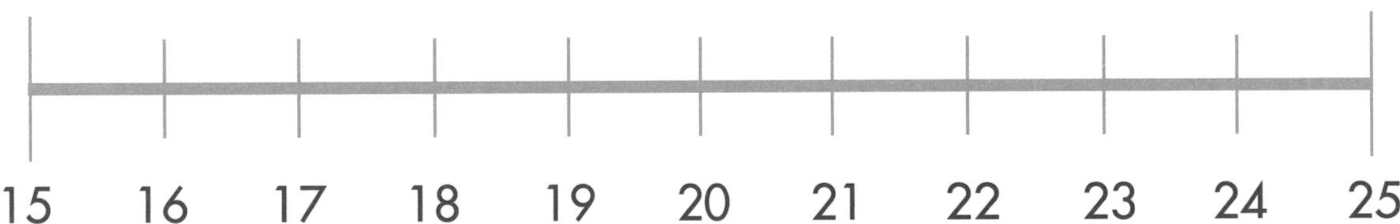

Lines of Symmetry

A shape that can be folded exactly in half is called symmetrical. The fold is a line of symmetry.

1. Draw one line of symmetry on these shapes.

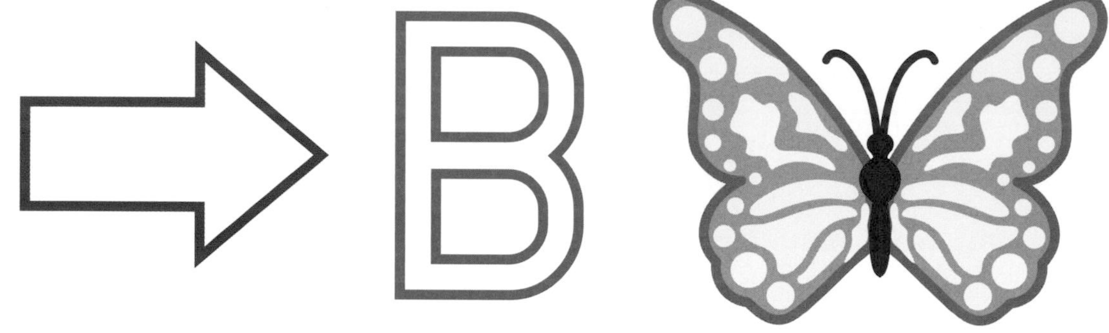

2. How many lines of symmetry does the letter H have?

3. Draw lines of symmetry on this regular pentagon. How many lines are there?

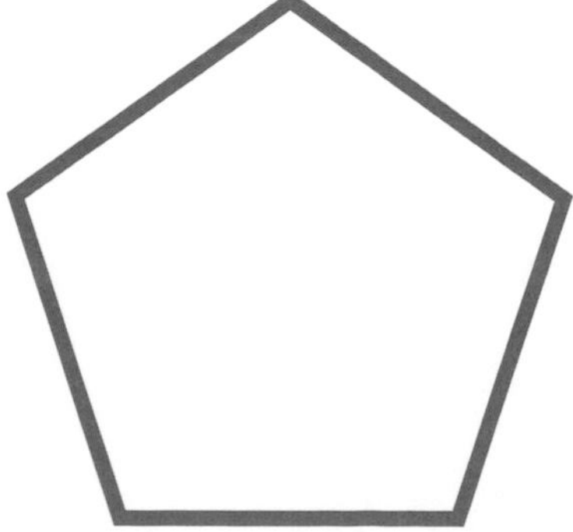

Time Filler:
Can you find 10 things around your home that have one or more lines of symmetry?

4) Circle the shape that is not symmetrical.

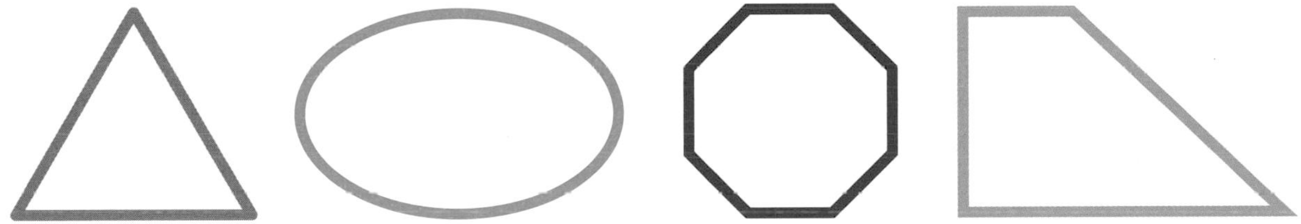

5) Complete the picture by drawing the other half.
Color the pattern so that it is symmetrical.

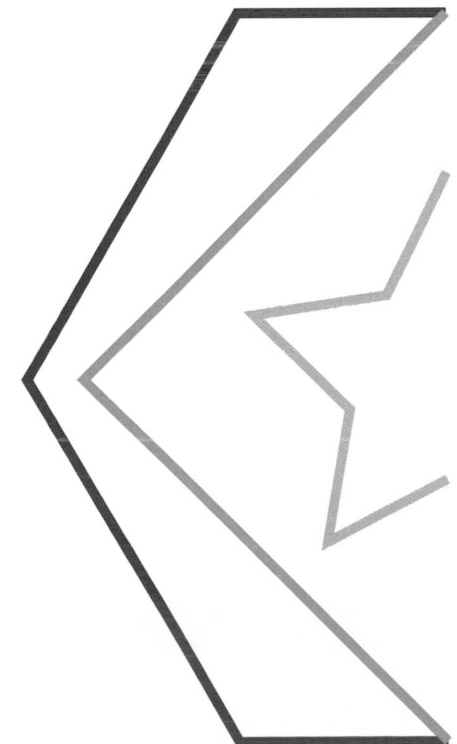

Beat the Clock 1

Write these numbers as digits. How many can you do in 10 minutes?

(1) Nine	(2) Twelve	(3) Twenty-two
(4) Sixteen	(5) Three	(6) Thirty-two
(7) Eight	(8) Four	(9) Eleven
(10) One	(11) Twenty-seven	(12) Thirty-eight
(13) Forty-three	(14) Eighteen	(15) Seven
(16) Fifty-six	(17) Thirty-three	(18) Fourteen
(19) Twenty-one	(20) Fifteen	(21) Forty
(22) Sixty-nine	(23) Eighty	(24) Fifty-three
(25) Twenty	(26) Forty-five	(27) Fifty-one
(28) Nineteen	(29) Five	(30) Sixty-four

Time Filler:
Have you checked your answers? How long did it take you? Check your answers. They are on page 80.

31 Eighty seven	32 Thirty	33 Forty-four
34 Eighty-two	35 Sixty-one	36 Forty-nine
37 Twenty-six	38 Fifty-five	39 Ten
40 Seventy-seven	41 Thirteen	42 Sixty-six
43 Ninety-eight	44 Seventy-three	45 Thirty-four
46 Eighty-one	47 One hundred	48 Twenty-five
49 Sixty	50 Ninety-five	51 Seventy-six
52 Eighty-four	53 Thirty-seven	54 Seventy-five
55 Eighty-eight	56 Ninety-two	57 Fifty-seven
58 Forty-eight	59 Sixty-two	60 Ninety-nine

Adding Numbers

"Total," "sum," and "altogether" all mean to add together the numbers given. Give it a try!

1) What is the total of 5 and 8?

2) Add together 12 and 16.

3) Add the following numbers:

40 + 20 = ☐

8 + 6 = ☐

48 + 26 = ☐

Time Filler:
Make two numbers with one or more of the digits 3, 2, and 5, such as 53. Now add the two numbers together. Make some more numbers by using the digits more than once, such as 33. Add these new numbers together.

(4) Complete these questions.

$$\begin{array}{r} 28 \\ +\ 11 \\ \hline \end{array} \qquad \begin{array}{r} 34 \\ +\ 25 \\ \hline \end{array} \qquad \begin{array}{r} 52 \\ +\ 37 \\ \hline \end{array} \qquad \begin{array}{r} 47 \\ +\ 19 \\ \hline \end{array}$$

....

(5) 32 children went to school in one bus and 27 children in another bus. How many children were there altogether?

Measuring Weight

These questions are all about weight.

1 Which is heavier? Check (✔) the answer.

☐ An elephant

☐ A dog

2 What would you use to weigh a person? Circle the answer.

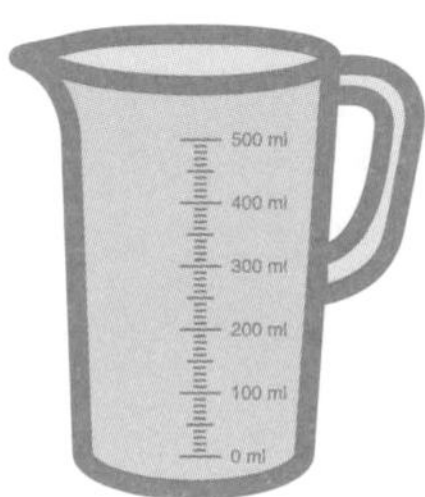

A measuring cup

Bathroom scales

3 Match the object with its weight. Draw a line.

	An apple	2 pounds
	A bag of sugar	1 ton
	A small car	4 ounces

Time Filler:
How much do some of your toys weigh? Use bathroom scales to find out. Ask an adult to help you.

4. Look at these scales. How much do these school books weigh?

5. Kia measured 4 ounces of butter into a mixing bowl and then added 8 ounces of sugar. What was the total weight?

Subtracting Numbers

"Difference," "take away," and "less than" mean to subtract the numbers given.

(1) What is the difference between 18 and 5?

(2) Take away 26 from 58.

(3) Subtract these numbers:

30 – 28 =

64 – 30 =

64 – 28 =

Time Filler:
Make two numbers with one or more of the digits 3, 2, and 4, such as 42. Now subtract the two numbers. Make some more numbers by using the digits more than once, such as 22. Subtract these new numbers.

(4) Complete these questions.

$$\begin{array}{r} 25 \\ -\ 13 \\ \hline \end{array}$$
....

$$\begin{array}{r} 38 \\ -\ 24 \\ \hline \end{array}$$
....

$$\begin{array}{r} 55 \\ -\ 37 \\ \hline \end{array}$$
....

$$\begin{array}{r} 47 \\ -\ 19 \\ \hline \end{array}$$
....

(5) Anya had a bag of 50 candies. She gave 28 candies to her friends. How many did she have left?

3-D Shapes

A three-dimensional shape is a solid shape. Are you ready to test your knowledge? Go!

1) Which shape is a cube? Check (✔) the answer.

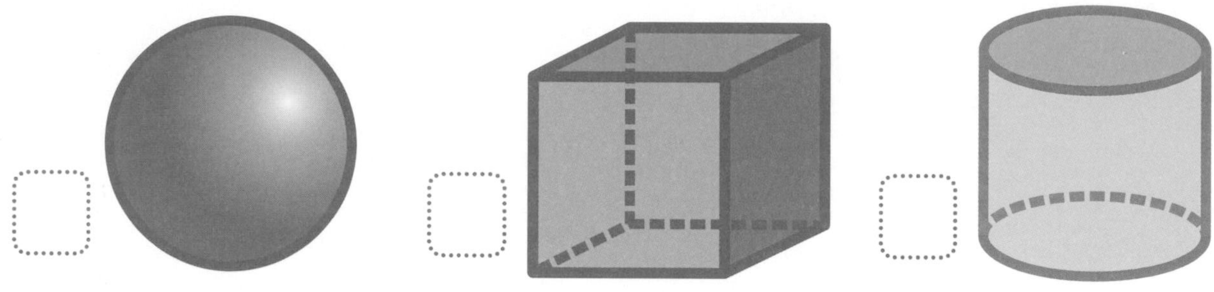

2) How many faces does a square-based pyramid have?

3) Match the shape to its name. Draw a line.

Triangular prism

Rectangular prism

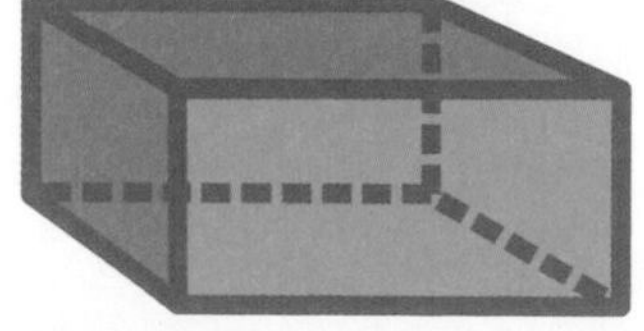

Cone

Time Filler:
Look around your home. Make a list of objects that are a sphere shape, a rectangular prism shape, or a cylinder shape. What other 3-D shapes can you find?

4) How many edges do these shapes have?

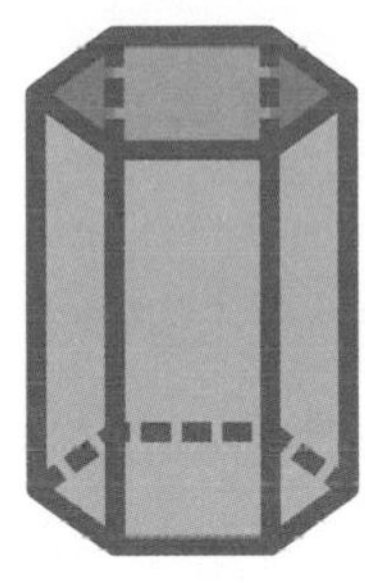

Hexagonal prism

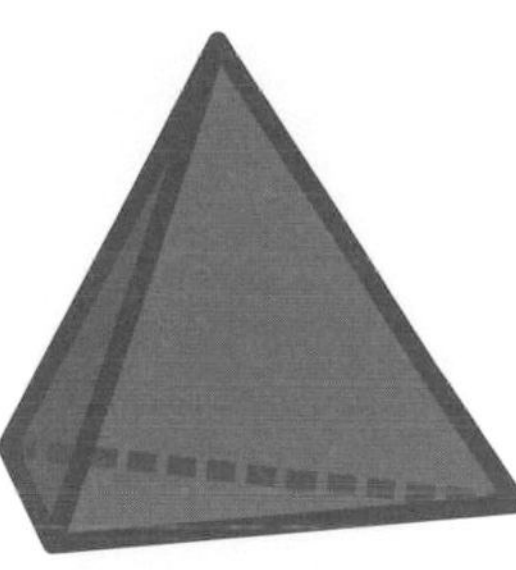

Triangle-based pyramid

Sphere

5) Which shape has the most vertices (corners)? Circle the answer.

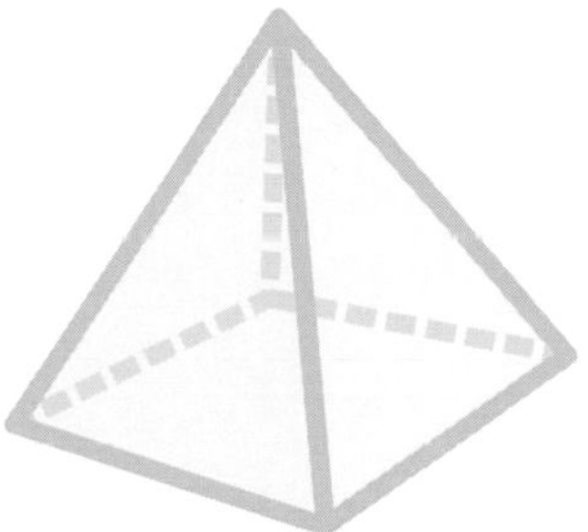

Sequences

Can you spot the number sequences? They can go either up or down.

1. Fill in the missing numbers.

6 10 14 ☐ 22 ☐ ☐

23 30 37 ☐ ☐ 58 

2. Circle the odd numbers in this sequence.

4 7 10 13 16 19

3. Fill in the missing numbers.

44 42 ☐ ☐ ☐ 34 ☐

73 70 67 ☐ ☐ 58 ☐

Time Filler:
Can you count up in even numbers from 2? Can you count up in odd numbers from 1?

(4) Write O for odd and E for even under each of these numbers.

40	33	26	19	12	5

7	45	62	84	29	38

(5) Fill in the missing numbers.

(+4)	13					33
(−3)	55					40
(−6)	36					6

Picture Data

Pictographs and graphs are useful ways to show information.

A farmer has 20 chickens. The pictograph shows how many eggs he collected each day for a week.

Eggs Collected Over One Week

Monday
Tuesday
Wednesday
Thursday
Friday
Saturday
Sunday

Key:
= 4 eggs
= 2 eggs

1. On which day did the farmer collect the most eggs?

2. How many eggs did the farmer collect on Tuesday?

3. How many more eggs did the farmer collect on Saturday than Sunday?

Time Filler:
Count how many times you and your family and friends can jump in two minutes. Draw a pictograph to show the results. What symbol will you use?

4) Look at the pictograph on page 32. Color in the blocks to show how many eggs the farmer collected each day.

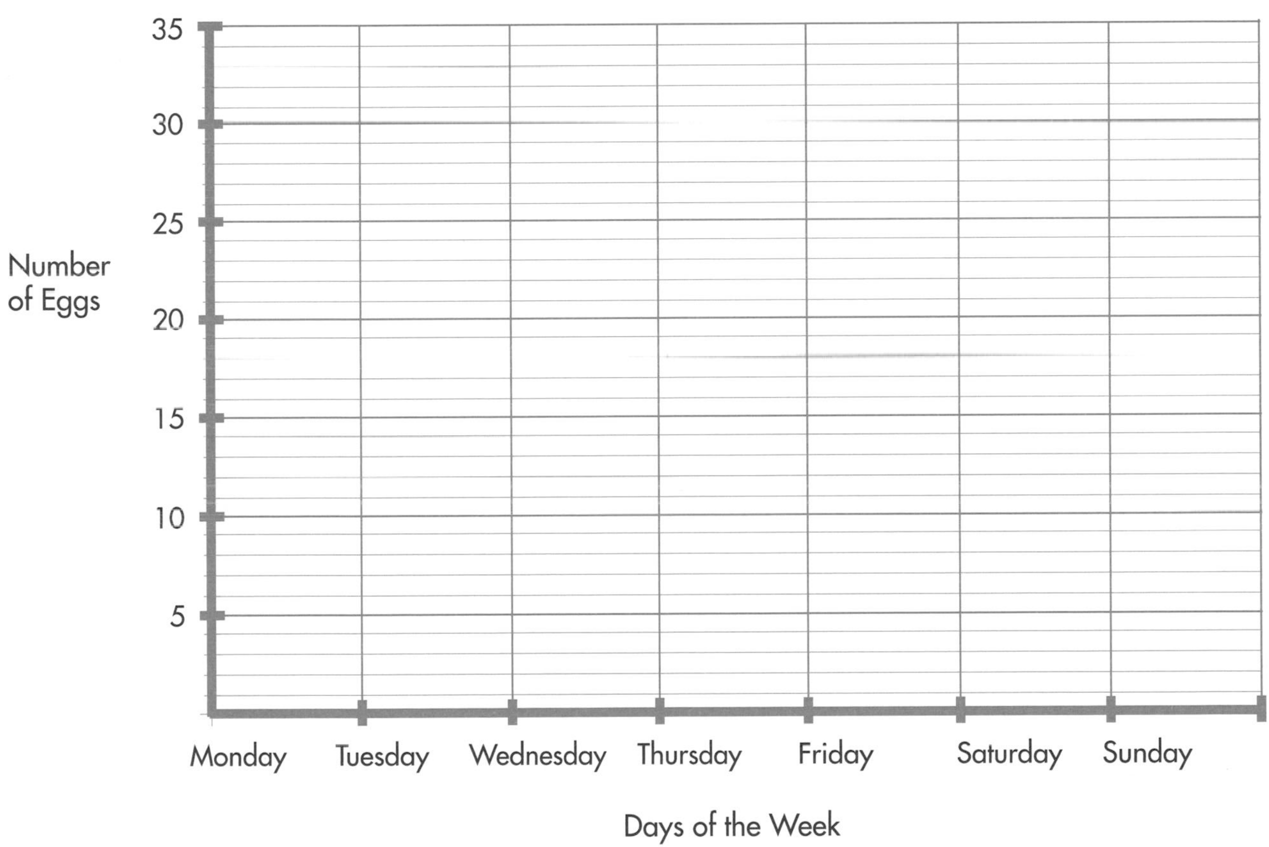

5) What is the total number of eggs collected on Wednesday and Thursday?

Patterns

Look carefully to complete these patterns. You will need some crayons.

1 Complete the pattern.

 .... 

2 Fill in the missing shapes.

 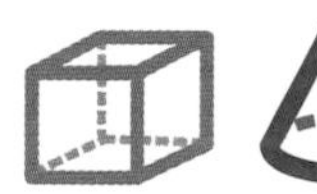   ....  ....

3 Complete the arrow pattern.

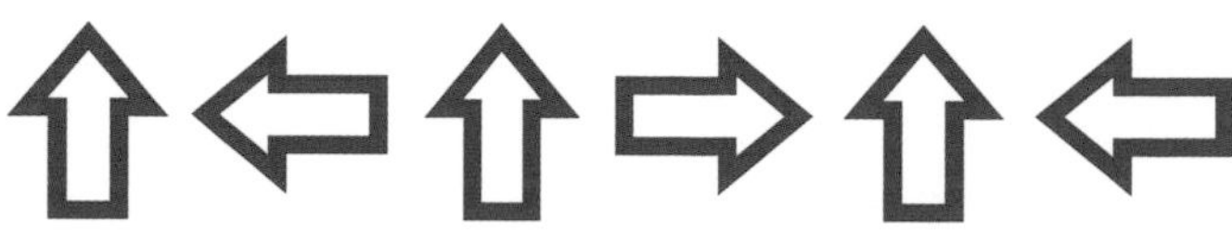 ....

Time Filler:
Design your own patterns. Use shapes, colors, and sizes to vary your patterns.

(4) Complete the pattern on the necklace.

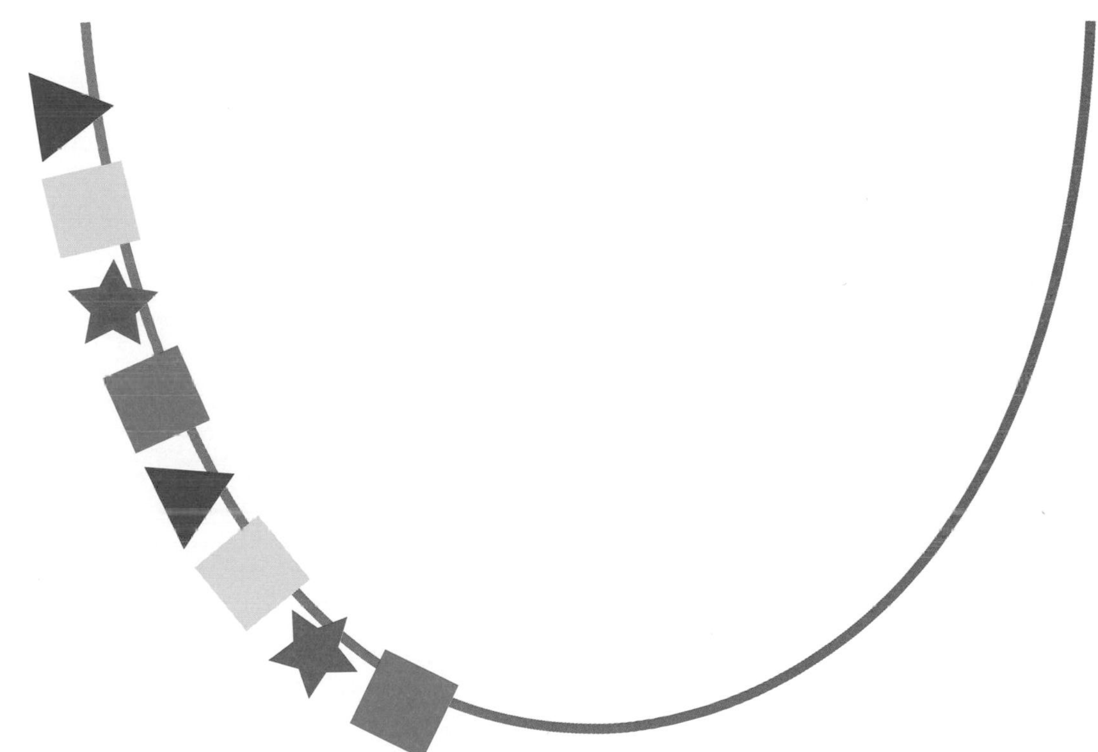

(5) Fill in the faces.

  ....  ....  ....

Rounding Numbers

Rounding a number to the nearest ten is a useful way to make a quick estimate.

(1) These numbers have ones place of 5 or more. Round them up to the next ten.

36 rounds up to

49 rounds up to

25 rounds up to

(2) Circle the numbers with ones place less than 5.

18 34 62 78 53

(3) Round these numbers down. Remember to keep the tens digit the same.

21 rounds down to

64 rounds down to

83 rounds down to

Time Filler:
Try estimating how many cookies are in a packet and how many candies are in a bag.

4) There are 11 blue candies, 24 yellow candies, and 9 green candies in a jar. Estimate to the nearest 10 how many candies there are.

5) Draw lines to connect the numbers on the left to their nearest 10 on the right.

27	
12	10
36	20
42	30
17	40
23	50
48	

Time Facts

It is time to be alert and ready to answer some questions all about time.

① Draw lines to connect the matching time facts.

Hours in a day	12
Days of the week	10
Months of the year	52
Years in a decade	24
Weeks in a year	7

② Circle the clock that says 8:30.

③ How many minutes are there in 1 hour?

Time Filler:
What can you do in ten minutes? Think of some activities, such as the number of pages of a book you can read or the number of times you can throw and catch a ball.

(4) Show these times on the clocks.

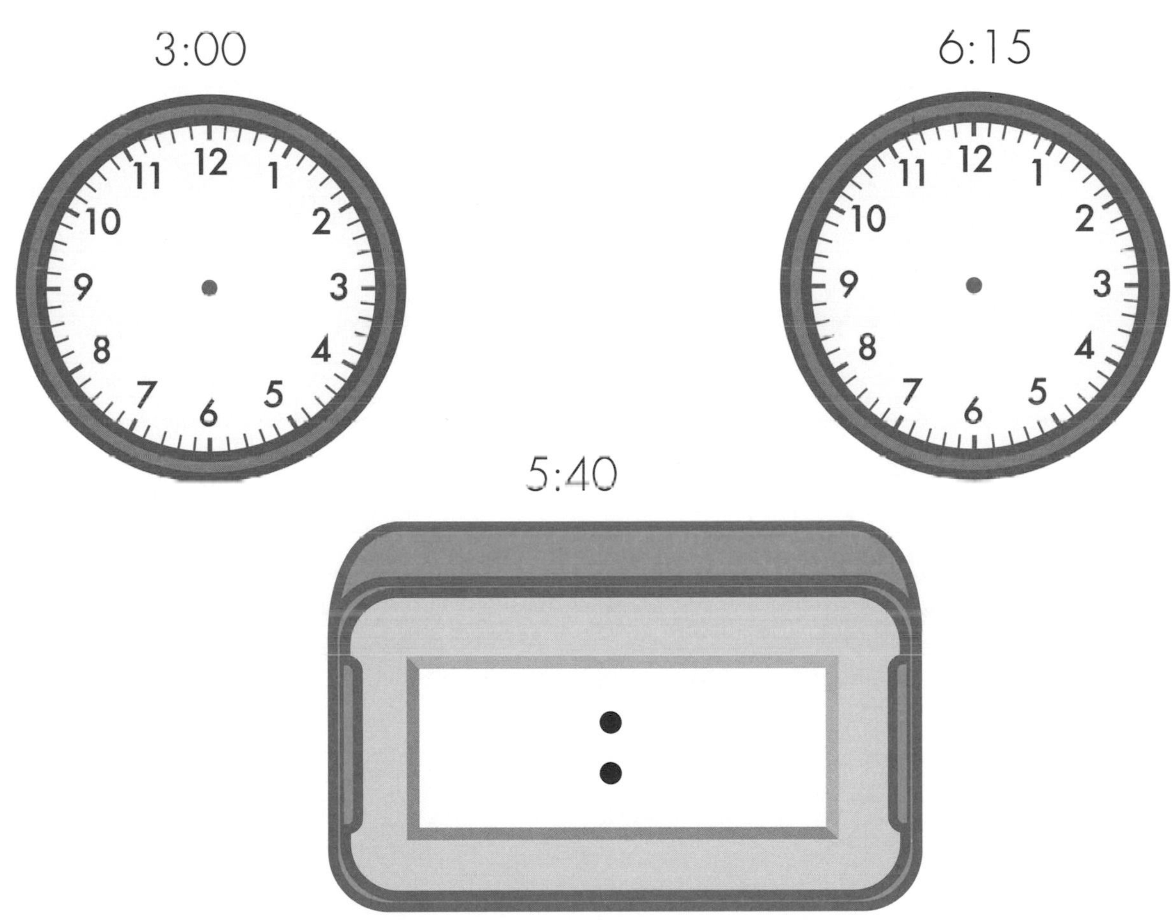

(5) The station clock says 2:20. The train arrives at 2:30. How long do the passengers have to wait?

Beat the Clock 2

Can you finish all these adding and subtracting problems in 10 minutes? Ready, set, go!

1. 2 + 7 =
2. 12 + 17 =
3. 22 + 27 =
4. 8 + 4 =
5. 18 + 24 =
6. 10 + 25 =
7. 32 + 15 =
8. 9 + 11 =
9. 19 + 41 =
10. 5 + 33 =
11. 9 − 4 =
12. 19 − 4 =
13. 29 − 14 =
14. 5 − 2 =
15. 45 − 12 =
16. 35 − 22 =
17. 64 − 33 =
18. 57 − 25 =
19. 27 − 15 =
20. 77 − 35 =
21. 66 + 14 =
22. 72 + 8 =
23. 21 + 19 =
24. 53 + 27 =
25. 48 + 12 =
26. 69 + 11 =
27. 24 + 56 =
28. 17 + 83 =
29. 30 + 70 =
30. 45 + 75 =

Time Filler:
Have you checked your answers? How long did it take you? Check your answers. They are on page 80.

(31) 8 – 5 =	(32) 28 – 15 =	(33) 58 – 35 =
(34) 7 – 2 =	(35) 57 – 22 =	(36) 87 – 42 =
(37) 6 – 5 =	(38) 36 – 15 =	(39) 96 – 25 =
(40) 56 – 45 =	(41) 7 + 4 =	(42) 57 + 64 =
(43) 5 + 9 =	(44) 45 + 29 =	(45) 6 + 8 =
(46) 76 + 18 =	(47) 9 + 9 =	(48) 49 + 39 =
(49) 7 + 8 =	(50) 47 + 18 =	(51) 13 – 7 =
(52) 33 – 17 =	(53) 15 – 8 =	(54) 55 – 28 =
(55) 14 – 6 =	(56) 84 – 46 =	(57) 11 – 4 =
(58) 31 – 24 =	(59) 71 – 44 =	(60) 100 – 95 =

Multiplying Numbers

"Times," "lots of," and "groups of" mean to multiply. These questions multiply by 2s, 5s, and 10s.

1. Mom has 2 baskets. Each basket has 4 apples. How many apples are there altogether?

2. What are 3 groups of 5?

3. Double these numbers.

3 5 7

Time Filler:
Multiplying is a quick way of adding. Look at a clock (not digital). Multiply each number by 5 and that will tell you how many minutes past an hour it is. Give it a try!

4. Complete these questions.

3 x 10 =

8 x 10 =

5 x 5 =

2 x 2 =

5. There were 4 flower pots. Each pot had 5 plants. How many plants were there altogether?

Measuring Liquids

These questions are all about measuring liquids.

1 Which holds the most liquid? Check (✔) the answer.

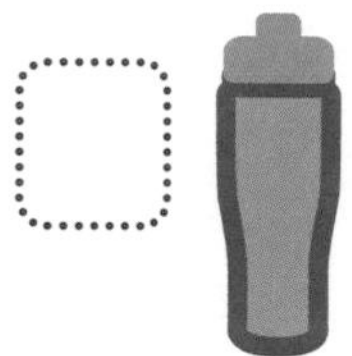

☐ A plastic bottle

☐ A watering can

2 What would you use to measure 200 ml of water? Circle the answer.

A measuring tape

A measuring cup

3 Match the object with its volume. Draw a line.

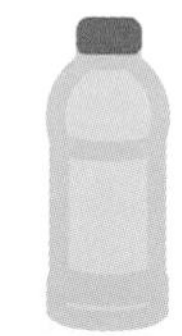

A small bottle of water

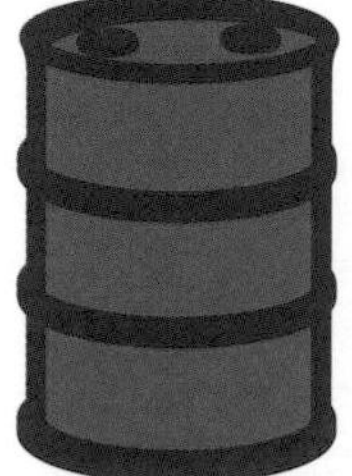

A barrel of oil

A large bottle of lemonade

2 pints

10 fluid ounces

40 gallons

Time Filler:
Fill some empty bottles of different sizes with water. Pour each one into a measuring cup to see how much water each bottle contained.

4) How much water is in these cups?

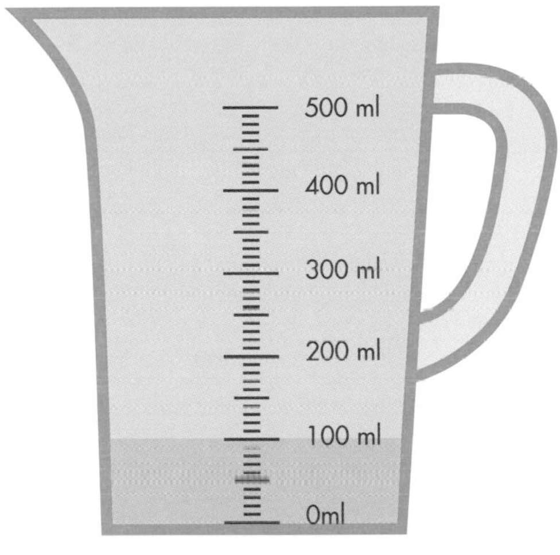

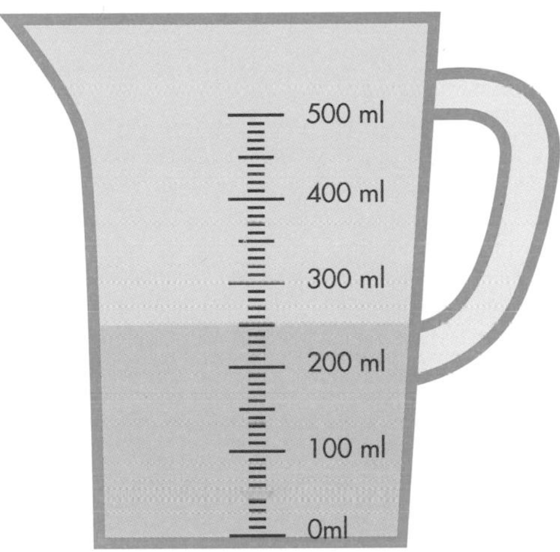

5) Connor filled up a jug with 50 ml of orange juice and then added 200 ml of water.

How much liquid was in the jug altogether?

Dividing Numbers

Knowing your 2, 5, and 10 times tables will help you work out these questions. Get set, go!

1. A pizza was cut into 8 slices. How many slices would 2 children each have?

2. What is 20 divided by 5?

3. Divide each of these numbers in half.

   8 14 22

Time Filler:
How many members are in your family? If you shared 20 candies equally, how many would you each get? Are there any candies left over?

(4) Complete these questions.

$40 \div 10 =$ ☐

$70 \div 10 =$ ☐

$35 \div 5 =$ ☐

$16 \div 2 =$ ☐

(5) A clown had 15 balloons to hand out equally to 5 children. How many balloons would each child get?

Directions

These questions are all about turns and position. Are you sitting comfortably? If yes, then give it a try!

1. Show where the arrow will point to if it makes a quarter turn counterclockwise.

2. Mark the right angles on this house.

3. Which compass direction is opposite North?

....

Time Filler:
Use a compass and explore your bedroom. What direction is your bed from the door—North, South, East, or West? What direction is your closet from the bed? Make a plan of your bedroom layout.

(4) Draw a circle in D1.

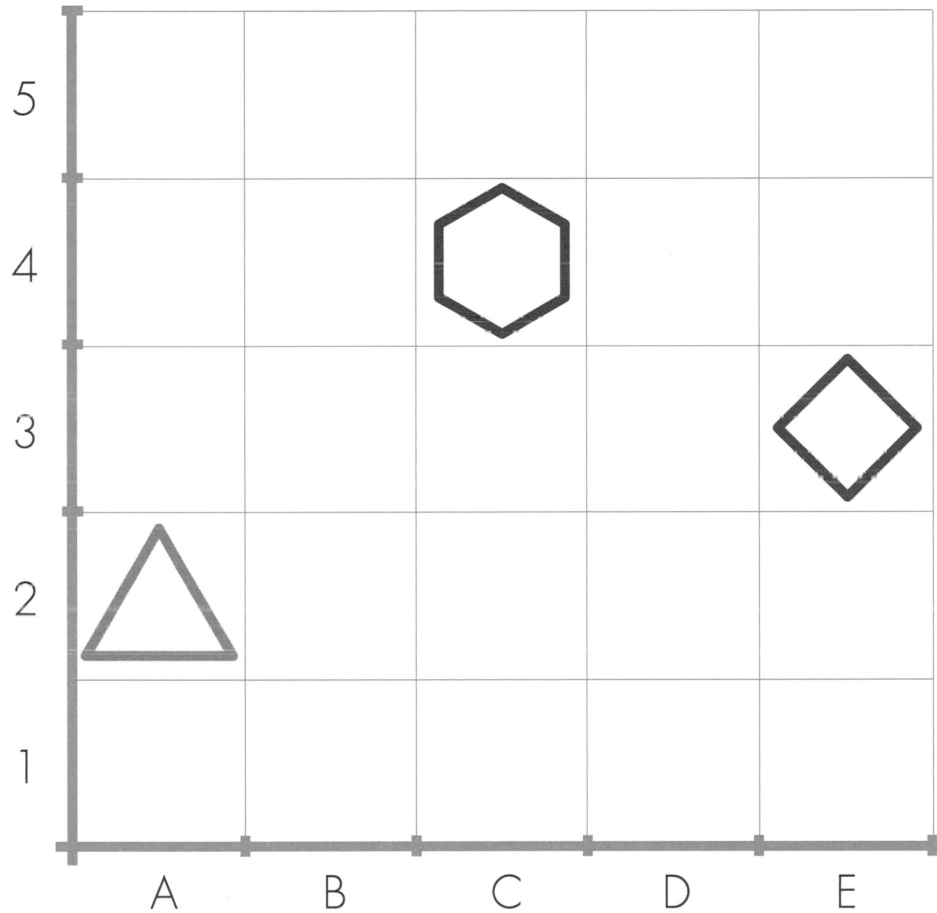

(5) What positions on the grid are these shapes?

Triangle ☐ Diamond ☐ Hexagon ☐

Times Tables

Do you know your 2s, 3s, 4s, 5s, and 10s times tables? If so, then you are ready to answer these questions.

1. Mark the number line counting in groups of 3.

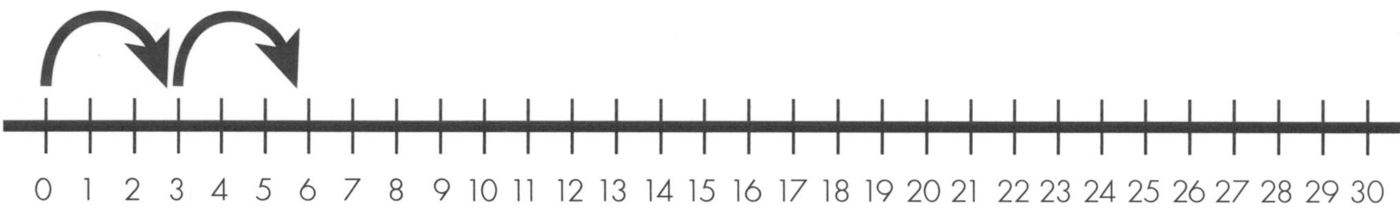

2. Complete the number sentence.

If 8 x 3 = 24, then 3 x 8 = ☐

3. Circle the multiples of 4.

12 21 28 35 40

Time Filler:
Did you know that any number multiplied by 0 gives the answer 0? Keep practicing saying those times tables and then you will be ready to move on to the 6x table.

④ Complete the multiplication square.

X	1	2	3	4	5
1		2		4	
2	2	4	6		10
3	3		9	12	
4	4	8	12		20
5		10		20	

⑤ Solve the questions.

5 x 2 = ☐ 7 x 2 = ☐

10 x 2 = ☐ 14 x 2 = ☐

5 x 4 = ☐ 7 x 4 = ☐

Diagrams

Carroll diagrams and Venn diagrams show how things are sorted into groups.

	Odd Numbers	Even Numbers
Less than 10	3	8
More than 10	21	14

(1) Add these numbers to the correct square in this Carroll diagram.

6 15 27 32

(2) In the diagram, which odd number is less than 10?

Time Filler:
Draw the Venn diagram below onto another piece of paper and add some other animals and 4-legged objects. How many can you think of?

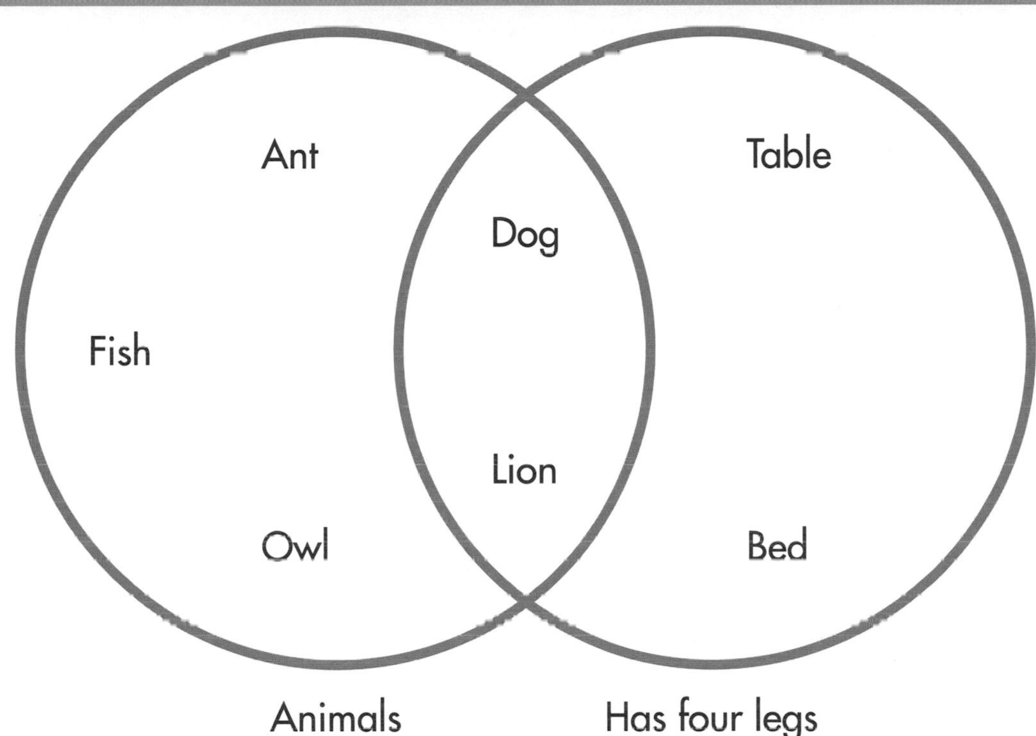

3) On this Venn diagram, which animals have four legs?

....

4) On this diagram, which animals do not have four legs?

....

5) Add a drawing of a chair onto the diagram.

Shopping

Getting to know all about using money is very helpful especially for when you go shopping.

1. Circle the three coins you would use to make 36¢.

2. A pencil costs 5 cents. How much would 3 pencils cost?

3. A pen costs 12 cents. How much change will you get from 25 cents?

Time Filler:
Set up your own store at home. Put price tags on objects around your house, and cut out pretend money from paper. As a storekeeper, you will be busy adding up the amounts and subtracting to find out what change to give.

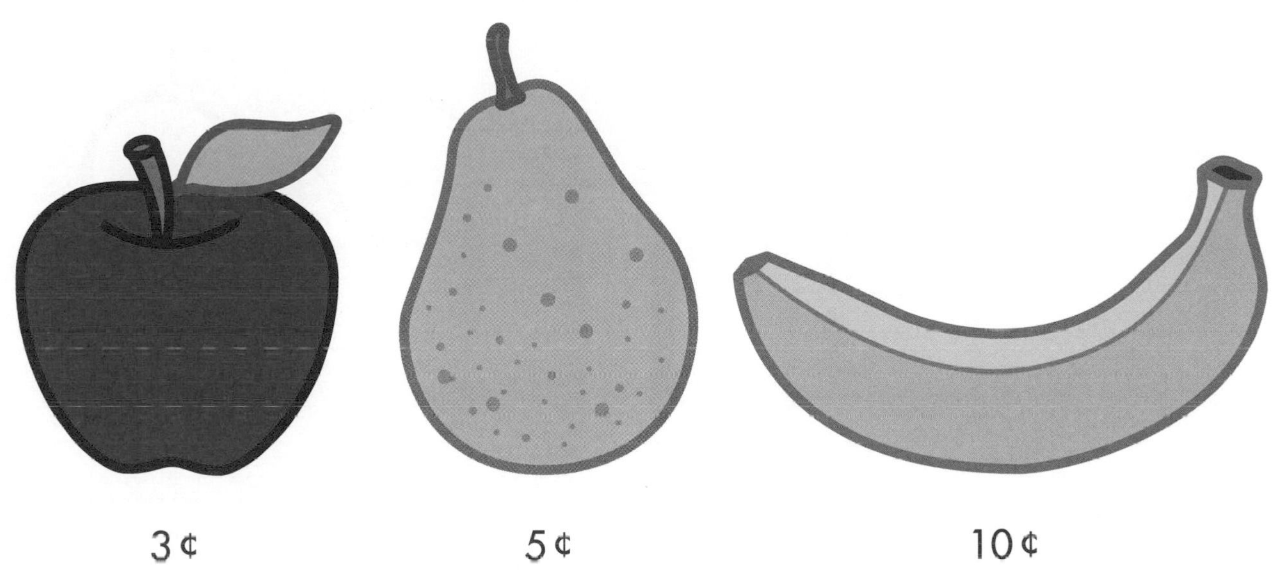

3¢ 5¢ 10¢

(4) How much will 3 apples and 1 pear cost?

(5) A woman buys 7 bananas. How much change does she get from $ 1.00?

Measuring Speed

Speed is measured in kilometers or miles per hour. How quickly will you zoom through these questions?

1. Which is faster? Circle the answer.

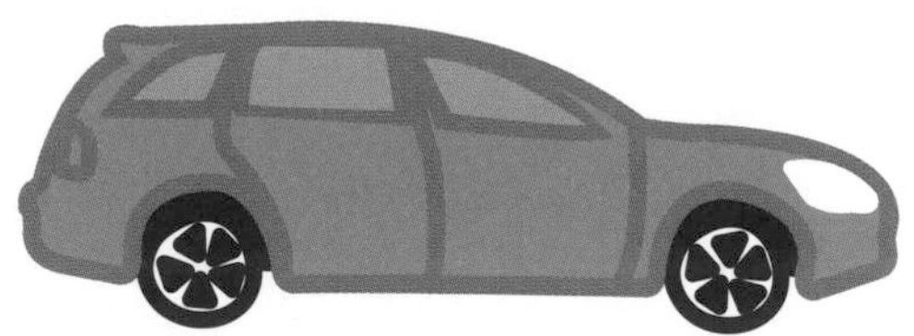

A car

A bicycle

2. What would you use to measure the speed of a runner? Circle the answer.

A stopwatch

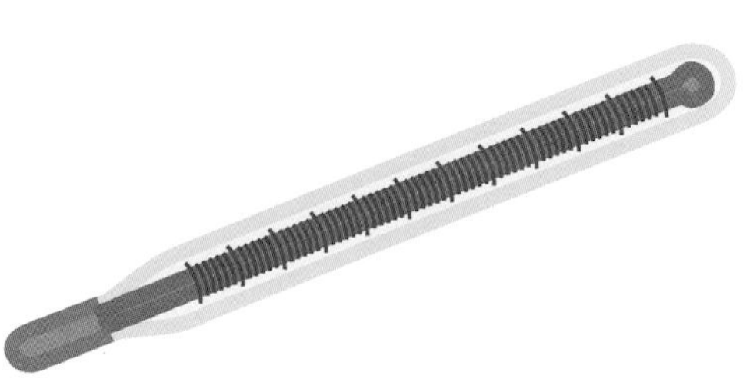

A thermometer

3. Match the object with its speed.

Racing car	70 miles/hr
Cheetah	4 miles/hr
A person walking	220 miles/hr

Time Filler:
Write down your top ten favorite animals. Put them in order of which ones you think will be the fastest to slowest movers. Ask an adult to help you find out the fastest speed of these animals. Was your estimated order correct?

④ Look at these times on the stopwatches. Which timed the fastest runner in a 1,000-yard race? ....

Runner 1

Runner 2

Runner 3

⑤ A cyclist traveled at 25 miles per hour along the road. He cycled at 12 miles per hour up a hill. How much slower did he cycle when going up the hill?

Problem Solving

Read these questions carefully to figure out if they are asking you to add, subtract, multiply, or divide.

1. There were 15 cookies. Jared ate 6. How many were left?

....

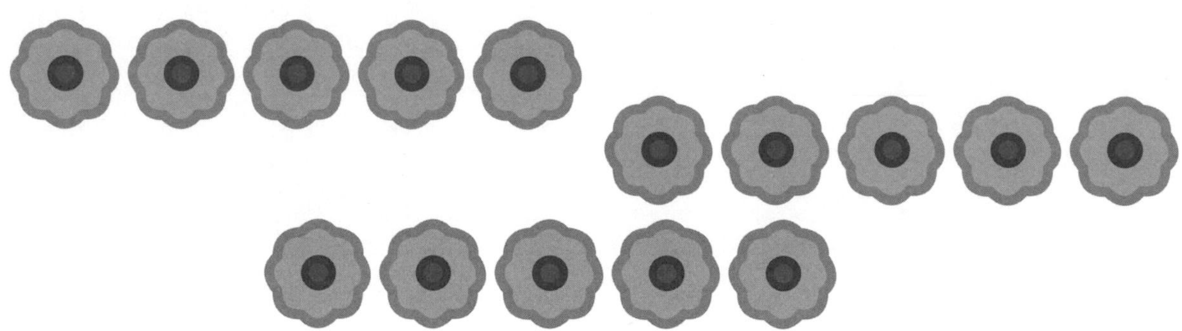

2. Mom had 13 mugs. She was given a set of 6 mugs. How many mugs did she have altogether?

....

3. There were 24 pieces of candy in a jar. They were shared equally between 3 children. How many candies did each child have?

....

Time Filler:
Think about how you have used math today. Have you been shopping or have you shared some candy? Have you cooked or checked the clock for the time?

(4) There were 5 bowls. There were 6 cherries in each bowl. How many cherries were there altogether?

....

(5) Ryan bought a pencil for 5 ¢, a notepad for 30 ¢, and an eraser for 12 ¢. How much change did he get from 50 cents?

....

More 3-D Shapes

Here are some more questions about comparing 3-D shapes.

1 Which is the net of a cube? Circle the answer.

2 Circle the shape with the most faces.

Triangular prism

Rectangular prism

3 Which shape has no edges? Circle the answer.

A sphere

A cylinder

Time Filler:
Find some empty tubes, boxes, and other recycled packaging. What sort of sculpture can you make by sticking them together?

(4) Label these shapes and count the vertices (corners).

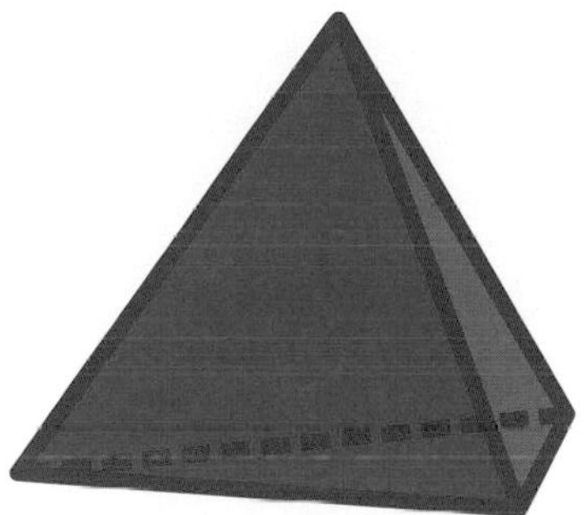

Name ....

Number of vertices ....

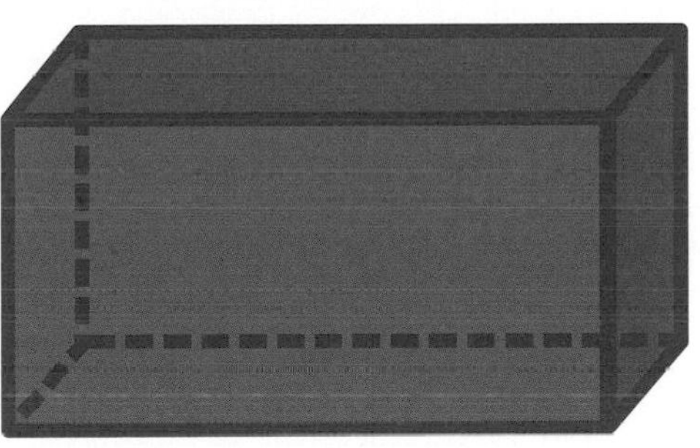

Name ....

Number of vertices ....

Name ....

Number of vertices ....

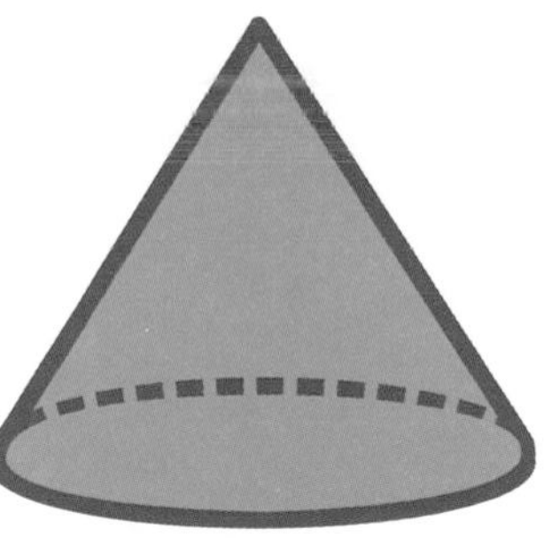

Name ....

Number of vertices ....

(5) Which shape has 2 bases, no vertices (corners), and 2 edges?

....

Fractions

A fraction is a part of a whole. You will need some crayons to do these questions.

1. Color in ¼.

2. Check (✔) the shape that shows ⅓.

3. How many halves are there in a whole?

Time Filler:
Draw around a circular plate on a piece of paper. Cut out the circle and then start folding it. Fold it in half, then quarters, then eighths, and then sixteenths. Between each fold, open up the circle and count the number of segments you have made.

(4) Here are 8 butterflies. Color in half of them.

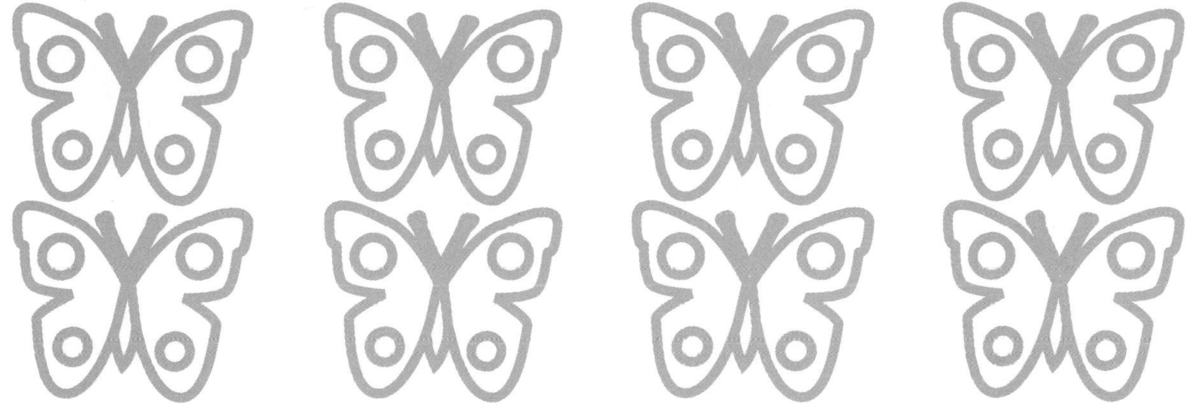

Fill in the answer: ½ of 8 = ☐

(5) Here are 12 balloons. Color a quarter of them.

Fill in the answer: ¼ of 12 = ☐

Beat the Clock 3

Can you finish all these questions in 10 minutes?

1. 2 x 2 =
2. 3 x 4 =
3. 4 x 3 =
4. 5 x 5 =
5. 6 x 2 =
6. 8 x 10 =
7. 9 x 2 =
8. 3 x 5 =
9. 2 x 7 =
10. 7 x 3 =
11. 20 ÷ 10 =
12. 12 ÷ 2 =
13. 9 ÷ 3 =
14. 8 ÷ 4 =
15. 50 ÷ 5 =
16. 22 ÷ 2 =
17. 16 ÷ 4 =
18. 16 ÷ 2 =
19. 3 ÷ 3 =
20. 8 ÷ 2 =
21. 4 x 2 =
22. 5 x 3 =
23. 7 x 1 =
24. 3 x 7 =
25. 1 x 11 =
26. 2 x 5 =
27. 5 x 4 =
28. 4 x 5 =
29. 6 x 3 =
30. 3 x 2 =

Time Filler:
Have you checked your answers? How long did it take you? Check the answers. They are on page 80.

(31) 10 ÷ 5 =	(32) 14 ÷ 2 =	(33) 40 ÷ 10 =
(34) 25 ÷ 5 =	(35) 4 ÷ 4 =	(36) 30 ÷ 5 =
(37) 60 ÷ 10 =	(38) 6 ÷ 2 =	(39) 15 ÷ 5 =
(40) 12 ÷ 3 =	(41) 5 x 7 =	(42) 8 x 2 =
(43) 9 x 1 =	(44) 10 x 10 =	(45) 4 x 7 =
(46) 6 x 4 =	(47) 4 x 8 =	(48) 3 x 9 =
(49) 10 x 8 =	(50) 3 x 3 =	(51) 18 ÷ 3 =
(52) 50 ÷ 10 =	(53) 40 ÷ 5 =	(54) 18 ÷ 2 =
(55) 30 ÷ 3 =	(56) 24 ÷ 4 =	(57) 45 ÷ 5 =
(58) 24 ÷ 2 =	(59) 110 ÷ 10 =	(60) 36 ÷ 4 =

Answers:

4–5 Place Value

6–7 Measuring Length

4

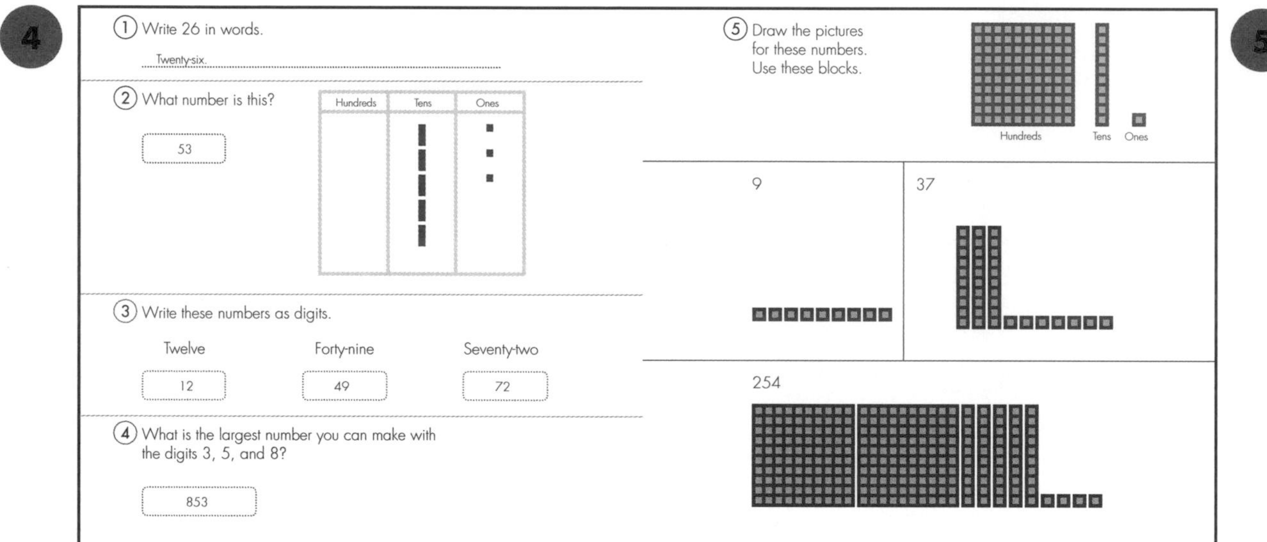

① Write 26 in words.

Twenty-six.

② What number is this?

Hundreds	Tens	Ones

53

③ Write these numbers as digits.

Twelve	Forty-nine	Seventy-two
12	49	72

④ What is the largest number you can make with the digits 3, 5, and 8?

853

⑤ Draw the pictures for these numbers. Use these blocks.

Hundreds Tens Ones

9

37

254

5

Working with hundreds, tens, and ones is an important part of early mathematical understanding. Although the spellings of some of the numbers are complicated, they will be very useful for your child to know. See pages 20–21 for some further number words to practice.

6

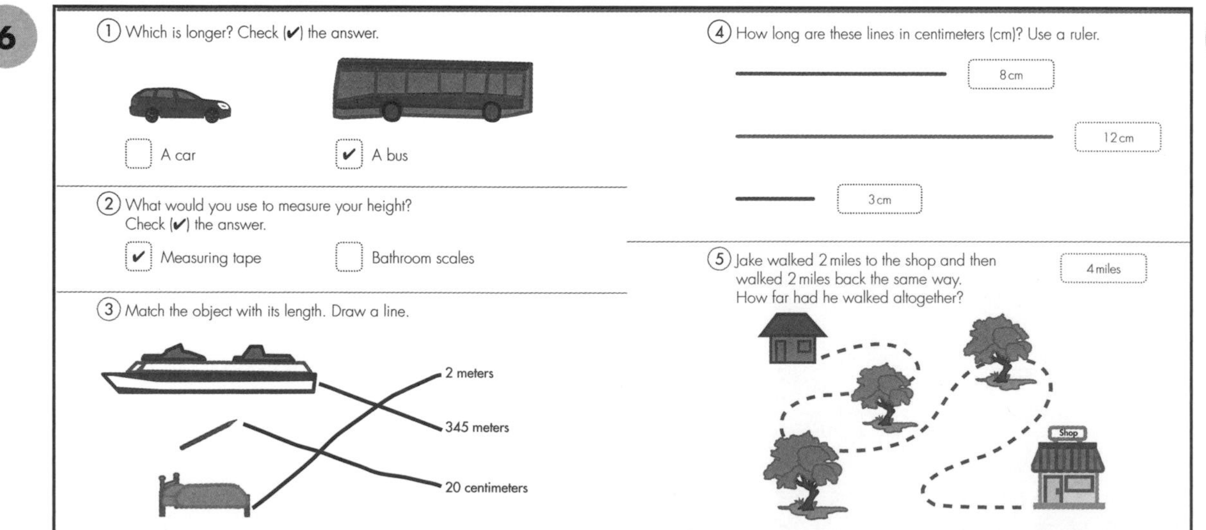

① Which is longer? Check (✔) the answer.

☐ A car ☑ A bus

② What would you use to measure your height? Check (✔) the answer.

☑ Measuring tape ☐ Bathroom scales

③ Match the object with its length. Draw a line.

2 meters

345 meters

20 centimeters

④ How long are these lines in centimeters (cm)? Use a ruler.

8cm

12cm

3cm

⑤ Jake walked 2 miles to the shop and then walked 2 miles back the same way. How far had he walked altogether?

4 miles

Shop

7

Help your child with these pages so that she/he becomes confident comparing and measuring lengths. At this stage, she/he is starting to be introduced to the units of measuring lengths, which can be confusing and daunting. When traveling, encourage your child to be aware of distances covered and begin to use the terminology.

Answers:

8–9 Counting

10–11 2-D Shapes

8

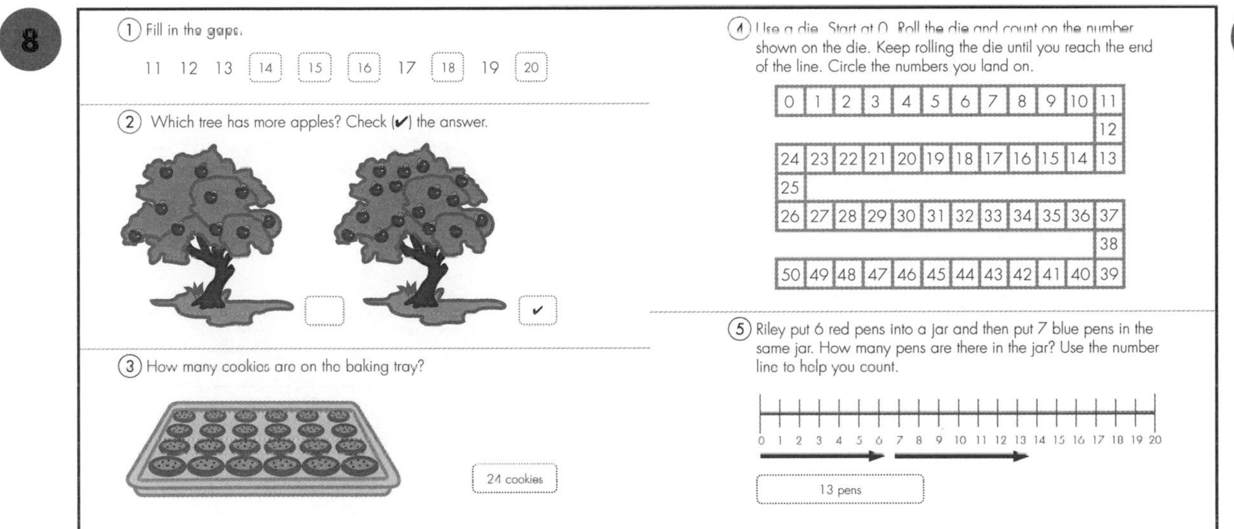

① Fill in the gaps.

11 12 13 14 15 16 17 18 19 20

② Which tree has more apples? Check (✔) the answer.

✔

③ How many cookies are on the baking tray?

24 cookies

④ Use a die. Start at 0. Roll the die and count on the number shown on the die. Keep rolling the die until you reach the end of the line. Circle the numbers you land on.

0 1 2 3 4 5 6 7 8 9 10 11 12 13 14 15 16 17 18 19 20 21 22 23 24 25 26 27 28 29 30 31 32 33 34 35 36 37 38 39 40 41 42 43 44 45 46 47 48 49 50

⑤ Riley put 6 red pens into a jar and then put 7 blue pens in the same jar. How many pens are there in the jar? Use the number line to help you count.

0 1 2 3 4 5 6 7 8 9 10 11 12 13 14 15 16 17 18 19 20

13 pens

9

Encourage your child to count objects at least up to 50. A number line will also help her/him identify the relationship and order of numbers. Playing board games with numbers are great for reinforcing counting practice.

10

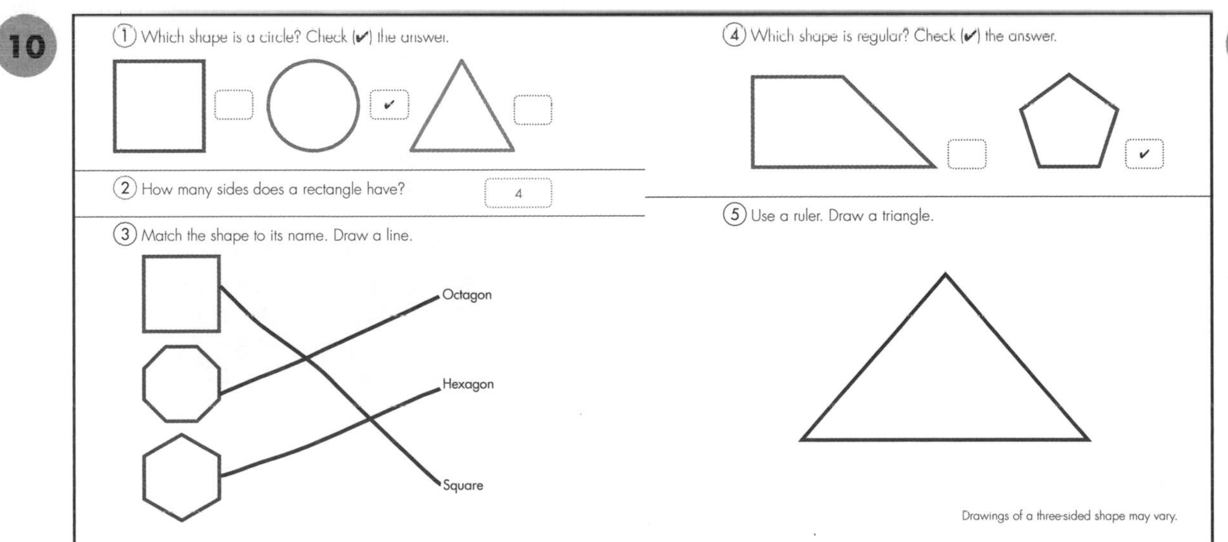

① Which shape is a circle? Check (✔) the answer.

✔

② How many sides does a rectangle have? 4

③ Match the shape to its name. Draw a line.

Octagon

Hexagon

Square

④ Which shape is regular? Check (✔) the answer.

✔

⑤ Use a ruler. Draw a triangle.

Drawings of a three-sided shape may vary.

11

Knowing the names and properties of 2-D shapes will help your child recognize the differences between them. Also she/he will need to be on the lookout for whether a shape is regular or irregular. Talking about the shapes around them, for example food packaging, will help too.

Answers:

12–13 Counting in Leaps
14–15 Tables and Charts

12

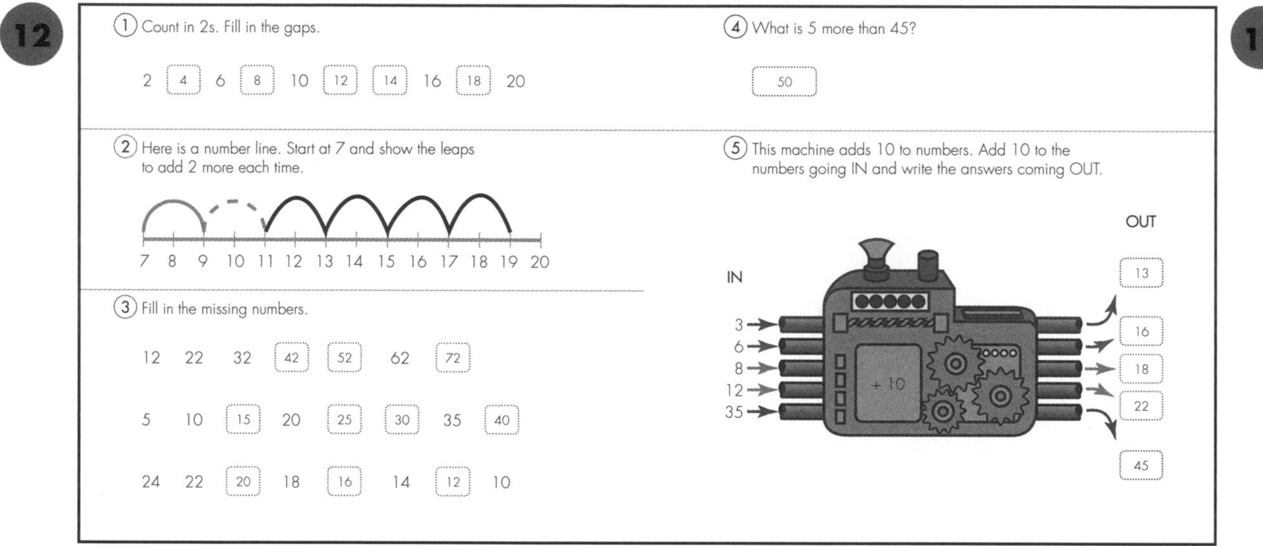

13

When counting in 2s, children should realize that if they begin on an odd number they will continue on odd numbers, and vice versa with even numbers.

For counting in 10s, the ones digits stay the same and only the tens digits go up.

14

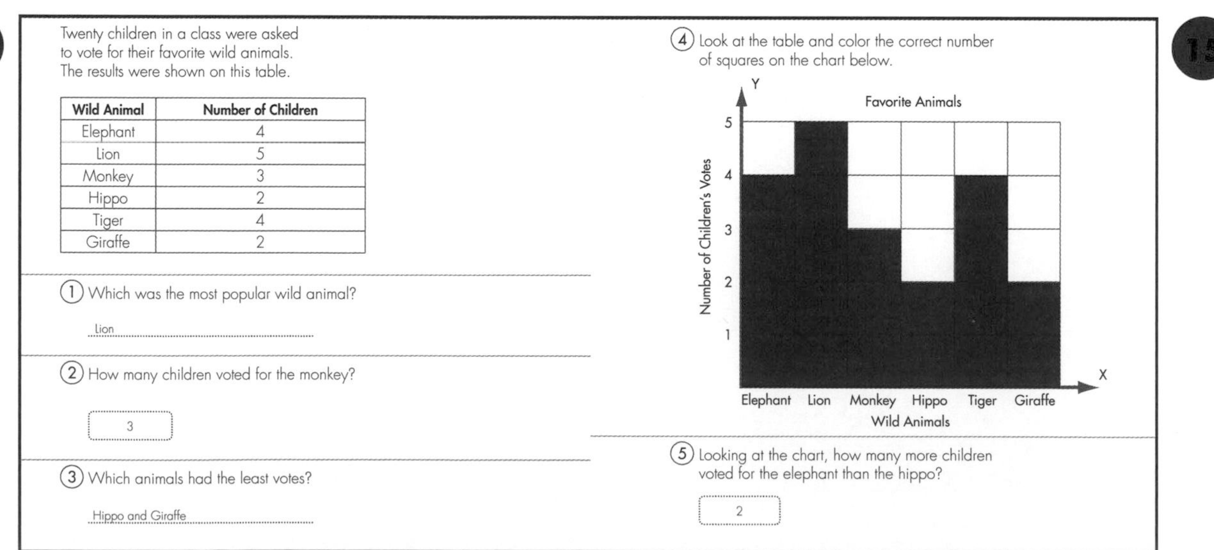

Twenty children in a class were asked to vote for their favorite wild animals. The results were shown on this table.

Wild Animal	Number of Children
Elephant	4
Lion	5
Monkey	3
Hippo	2
Tiger	4
Giraffe	2

15

Techniques for reading simple grids will help children with complex ones later. To create the chart on page 15 by coloring the correct number of squares, your child may like to use a different color for each animal.

Answers:

16–17 Number Order
18–19 Lines of Symmetry

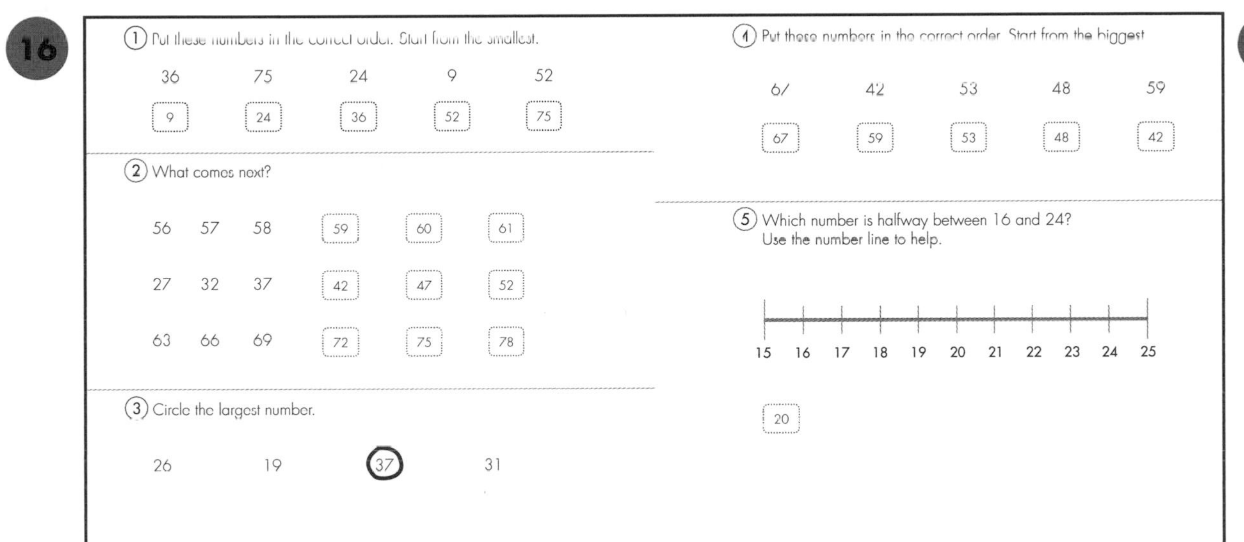

Arranging numbers in order helps to reinforce confidence in the value and concept of numbers. Check that your child is not reading and writing the numbers in reverse, such as 76 instead of 67. This indicates that they may need more practice on place value.

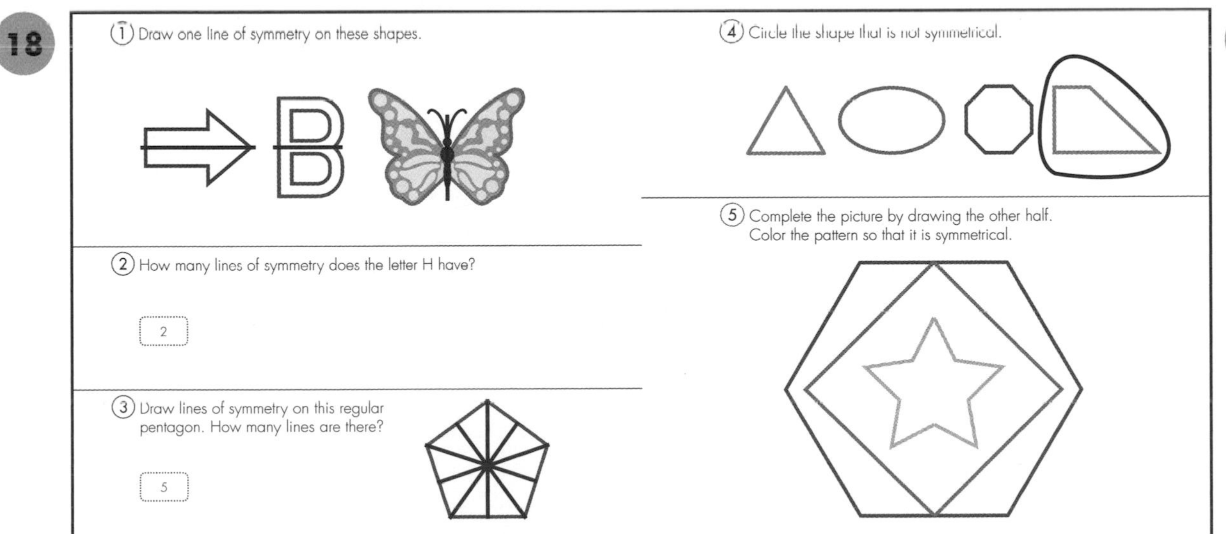

Is your child able to explain what a line of symmetry is? If they are finding this activity difficult, they could draw and cut out shapes on paper and fold them in half to see if they match and have any lines of symmetry. Putting a small mirror along the half-way line will also help show how the other half will match.

Answers:

22–23 Adding Numbers
24–25 Measuring Weight

22

1. What is the total of 5 and 8?

13

2. Add together 12 and 16.

28

3. Add the following numbers:

40 + 20 = 60

8 + 6 = 14

48 + 26 = 74

23

4. Complete these questions.

28	34	52	47
+ 11	+ 25	+ 37	+ 19
39	59	89	66

5. 32 children went to school in one bus and 27 children in another bus. How many children were there altogether?

59

Encourage your child to look for ways to make the calculations easier. Knowing single-digit number bonds such as 5 + 6, 6 + 7, and 7 + 8 are very useful. If she/he is adding a number to the digit 9, it is easier to add 10 and then take away 1. These strategies will be useful for mental arithmetic skills too.

24

25

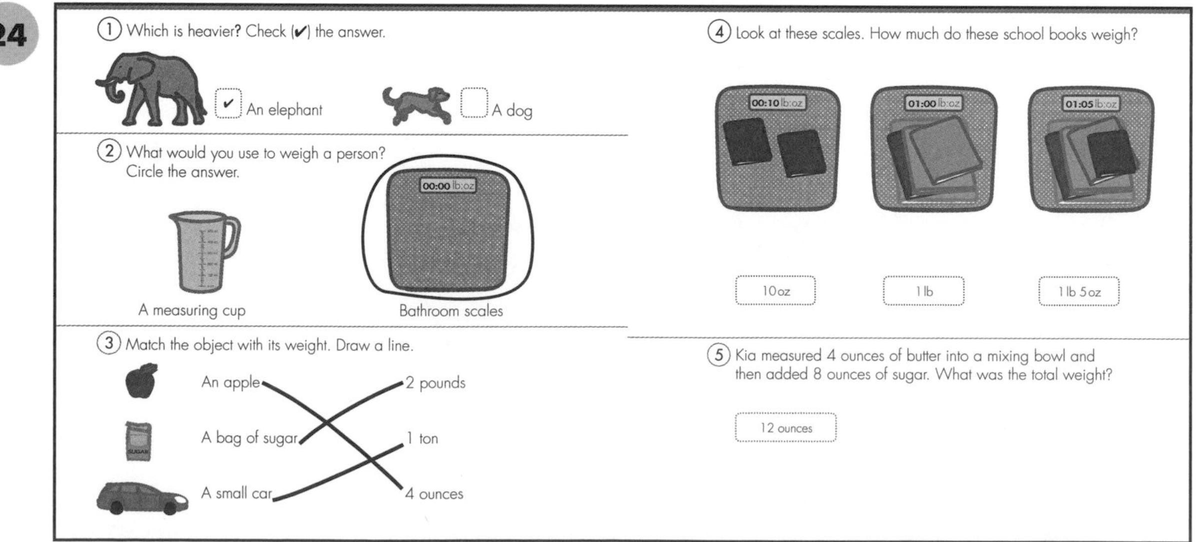

1. Which is heavier? Check (✔) the answer.

✔ An elephant

A dog

2. What would you use to weigh a person? Circle the answer.

A measuring cup

Bathroom scales

3. Match the object with its weight. Draw a line.

An apple — 4 ounces

A bag of sugar — 2 pounds

A small car — 1 ton

4. Look at these scales. How much do these school books weigh?

10oz

1lb

1lb 5oz

5. Kia measured 4 ounces of butter into a mixing bowl and then added 8 ounces of sugar. What was the total weight?

12 ounces

Towards the end of Grade 2, your child will begin to be introduced to units of weight. Encourage your child to help you weigh out produce on the scales in supermarkets. Also if possible, allow them to measure the weight of fruits and vegetables for fun.

Answers:

26–27 Subtracting Numbers
28–29 3-D Shapes

26

① What is the difference between 18 and 5?

13

② Take away 26 from 58.

32

③ Subtract these numbers:

30 – 28 = 2

64 – 30 = 34

64 – 28 = 36

④ Complete these questions.

25	38	55	47
– 13	– 24	– 37	– 19
12	14	18	28

⑤ Anya had a bag of 50 candies. She gave 28 candies to her friends. How many did she have left?

22

27

Let your child use a number line to help them calculate the answers if they need help visualizing. Encourage them to subtract the ones first and then move on to the tens. There is space around the questions for the children to show their workings or set the problem out in a way that works for them.

28

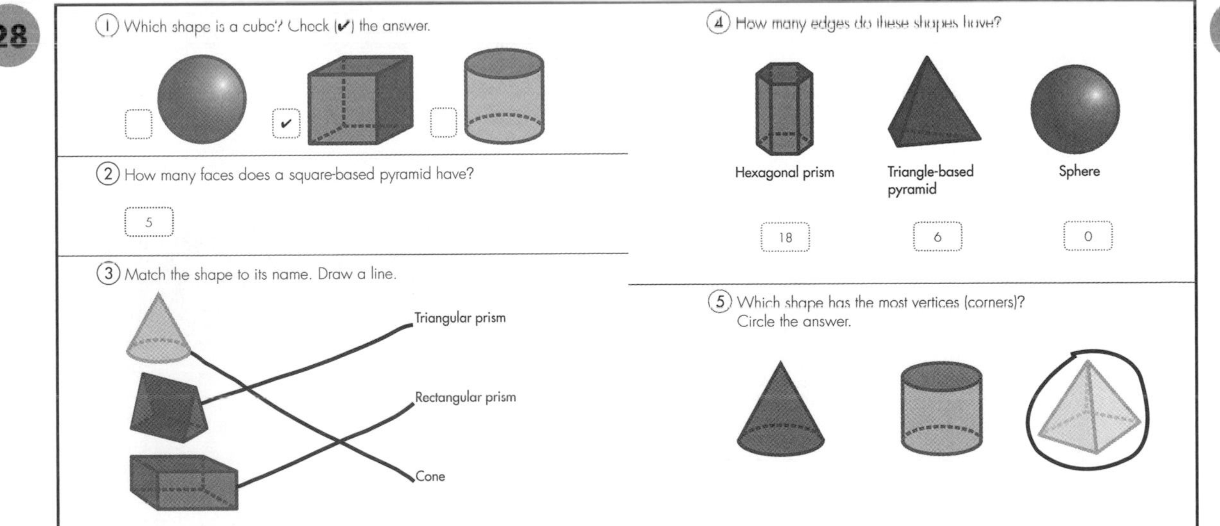

29

When discussing 3-D shapes, your child should start using mathematical language such as curved and flat faces, straight edges, and corners to describe and compare them. Encourage your child to find the shapes featured on the page at home so that she/he can feel the shape too.

Answers:

30–31 Sequences
32–33 Picture Data

30

① Fill in the missing numbers.

6 10 14 [18] 22 [26] [30]

23 30 37 [44] [51] 58 [65]

② Circle the odd numbers in this sequence.

4 (7) 10 (13) 16 (19)

③ Fill in the missing numbers.

44 42 [40] [38] [36] 34 [32]

73 70 67 [64] [61] 58 [55]

31

④ Write O for odd and E for even under each of these numbers.

40	33	26	19	12	5
E	O	E	O	E	O

7	45	62	84	29	38
O	O	E	E	O	E

⑤ Fill in the missing numbers.

(+4) 13 [17] [21] [25] [29] 33

(−3) 55 [52] [49] [46] [43] 40

(−6) 36 [30] [24] [18] [12] 6

Your child needs to first look out for the rule that works through each sequence. Creating their own sequences will also help them to understand and recognize relationships between the order of numbers.

32

A farmer has 20 chickens. The pictograph shows how many eggs he collected each day for a week.

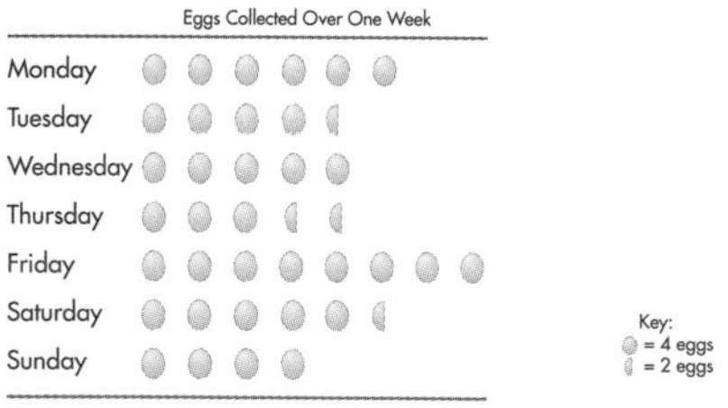

Eggs Collected Over One Week

Monday
Tuesday
Wednesday
Thursday
Friday
Saturday
Sunday

Key:
= 4 eggs
= 2 eggs

① On which day did the farmer collect the most eggs?

Friday

② How many eggs did the farmer collect on Tuesday?

[18]

③ How many more eggs did the farmer collect on Saturday than Sunday?

[6]

33

④ Look at the pictograph on page 32. Color in the blocks to show how many eggs the farmer collected each day.

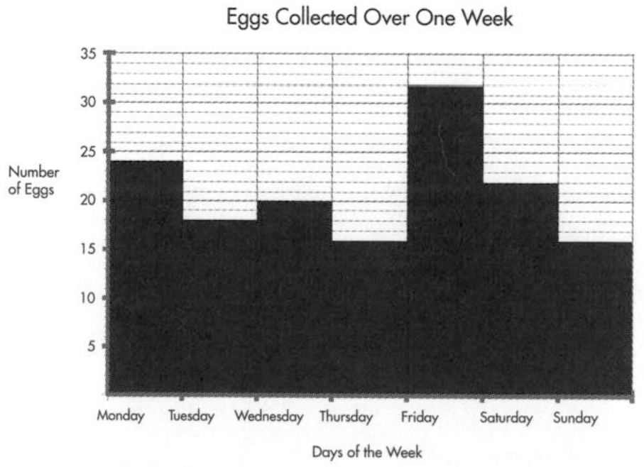

Eggs Collected Over One Week

Number of Eggs: 5, 10, 15, 20, 25, 30, 35

Monday Tuesday Wednesday Thursday Friday Saturday Sunday

Days of the Week

⑤ What is the total number of eggs collected on Wednesday and Thursday?

[36]

Pictographs are a fun visual way of presenting data. Make sure that your child notices the key, where one egg image represents four eggs and half an egg image represents two eggs. Encourage your child to work out the number of eggs collected for each day at the beginning.

Answers:

34–35 Patterns
36–37 Rounding Numbers

34 35

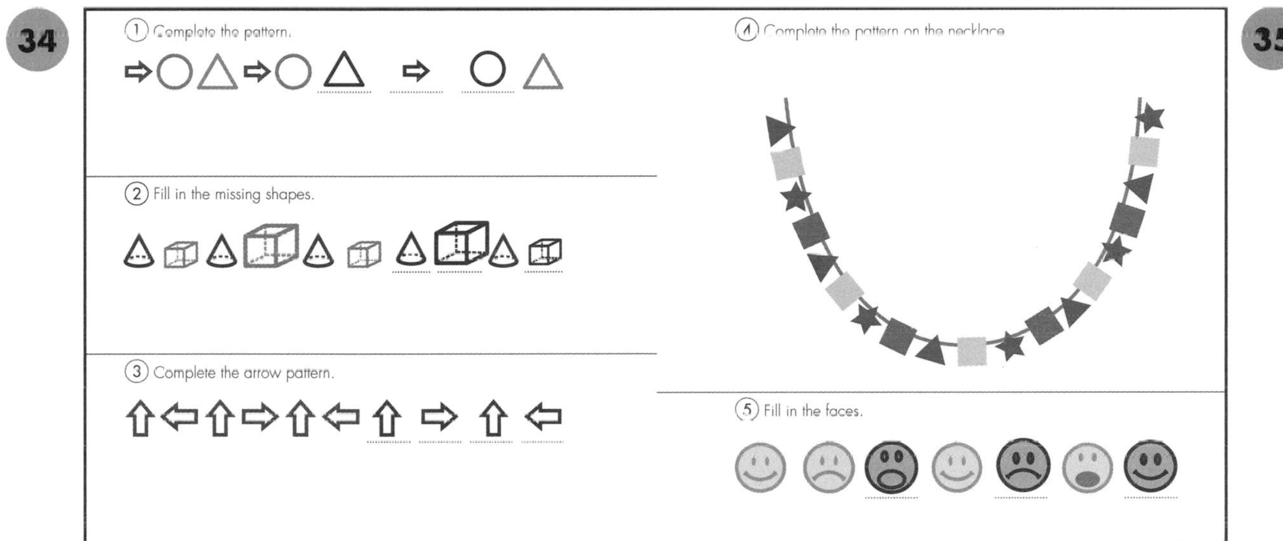

Spotting patterns made with different shapes, sizes, positions, and colors is a fun way of developing ordering skills. Encourage your child to describe the patterns she/he creates using mathematical language such as bigger, smaller, circles, squares, left or right arrow, and up and down.

36 37

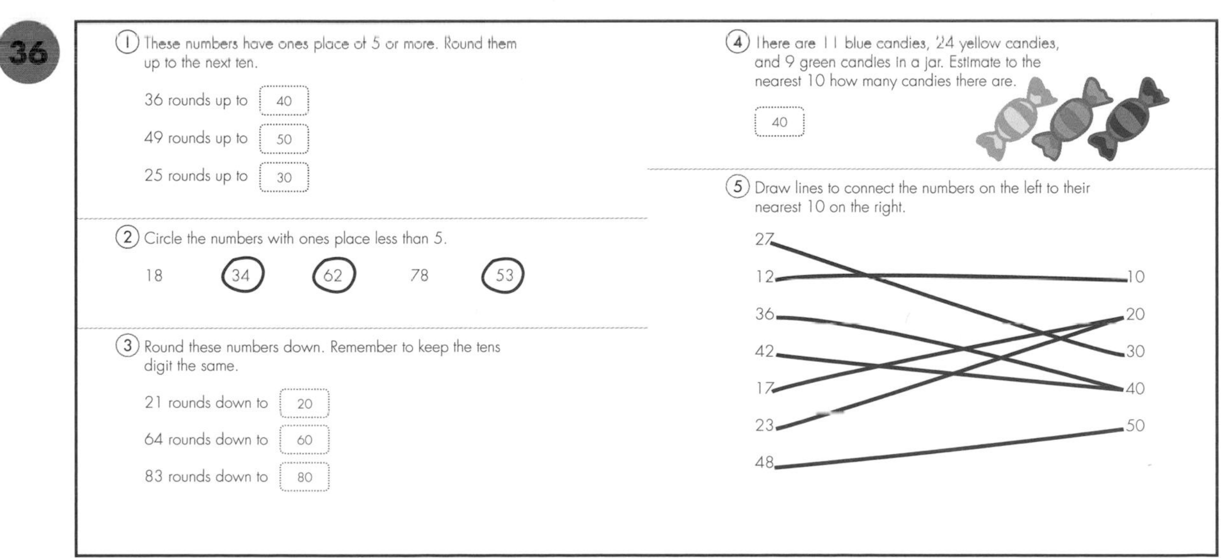

Remind your child to keep the tens the same if rounding down when the ones are less than 5 and increase the tens if the ones are 5 or more. Explain that rounding is a useful way of estimating answers. Your child could practice rounding when shopping to quickly estimate the total price of one or two things.

Answers:

38–39 Time Facts
42–43 Multiplying Numbers

38

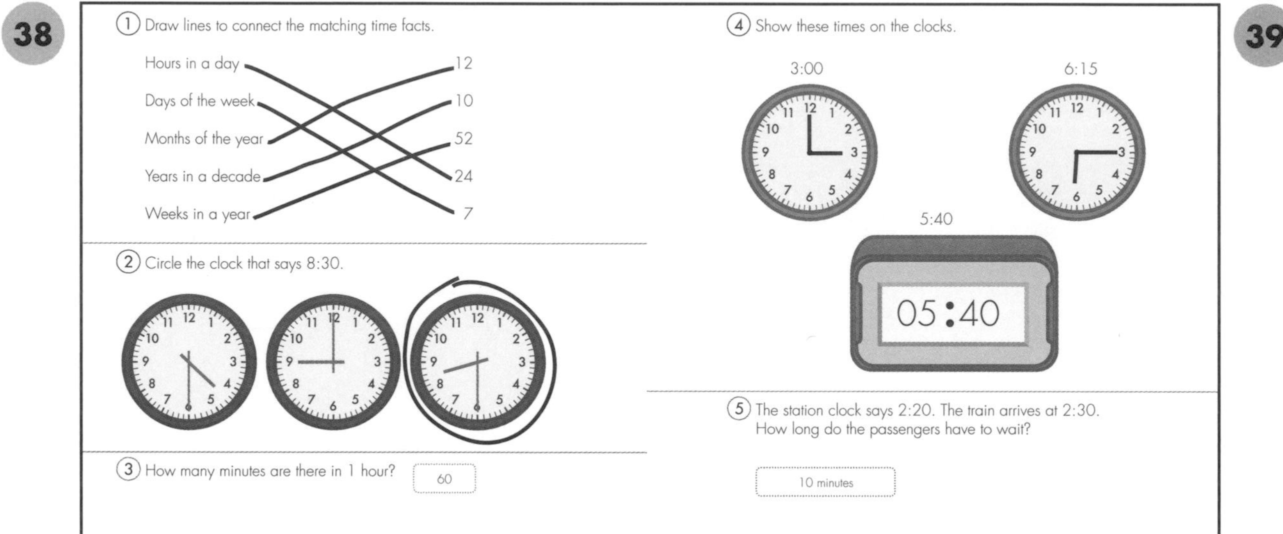

39

Point out to your child how the little hour hand on a clock moves on slowly. Its slightly changed position is important to show at the half past and quarter past. Encourage your child to practice saying the days of the week and months of the year in the correct order.

42

1. Mom has 2 baskets. Each basket has 4 apples. How many apples are there altogether?

   8

2. What are 3 groups of 5?

   15

3. Double these numbers.

3	5	7
6	10	14

43

4. Complete these questions.

   3 x 10 = 30

   8 x 10 = 80

   5 x 5 = 25

   2 x 2 = 4

5. There were 4 flower pots. Each pot had 5 plants. How many plants were there altogether?

   20

Your child needs to be familiar with the 2x, 5x, and 10x tables before progressing with these pages. If your child needs to visualize the question, encourage her/him to draw sets such as 2 baskets with 4 apples in each, or 3 piles of 5 candies for question 2.

Answers:

44–45 Measuring Liquids
46–47 Dividing Numbers

44 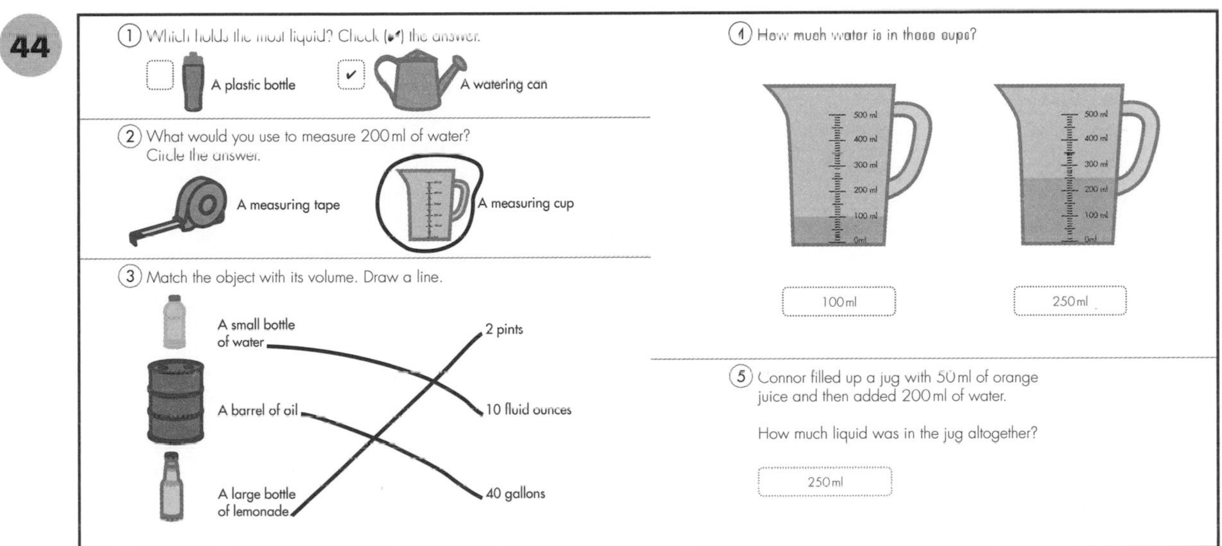 45

Your child will need your help as they answer these questions about units of measuring liquids. Encourage your child to fill different-sized containers with water and then pour the amount into a measuring cup to see the amount, or help you pour certain amounts of water, milk, or other liquids during cooking.

46 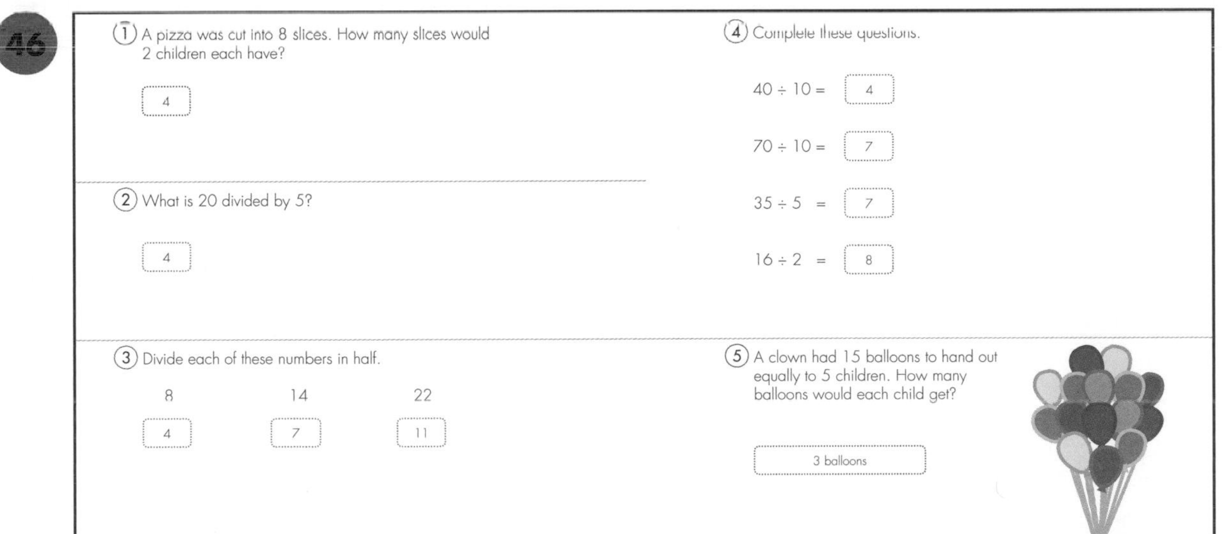 47

Just like on pages 42–43, encourage your child to visualize the questions by drawing piles of candies or coins and then distributing them out into the right number of groups in the space provided. Look out for opportunities which require sharing an equal number, for example sharing candies in a bag among the family.

Answers:

48–49 Directions
50–51 Times Tables

48

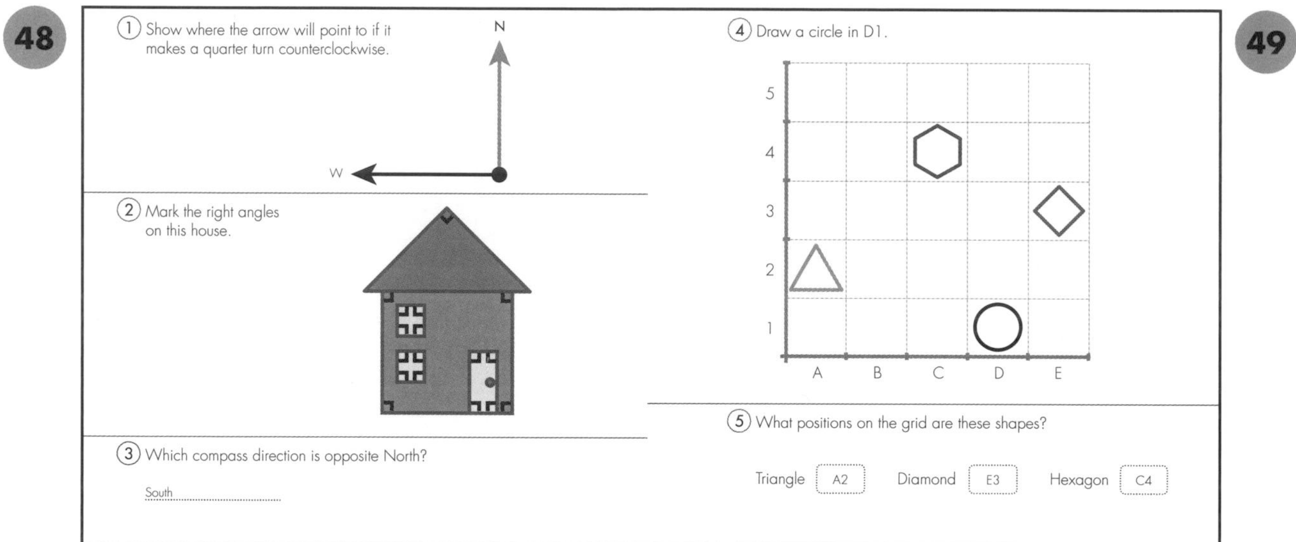

(1) Show where the arrow will point to if it makes a quarter turn counterclockwise.

(2) Mark the right angles on this house.

(3) Which compass direction is opposite North?

South

(4) Draw a circle in D1.

(5) What positions on the grid are these shapes?

Triangle A2 Diamond E3 Hexagon C4

49

These questions are a mixture of challenges to encourage your child to think about position and turns. Show your child a compass and get out a few maps to show how the grid numbering works. Work out together the grid references of certain places and plan routes using directional language.

50

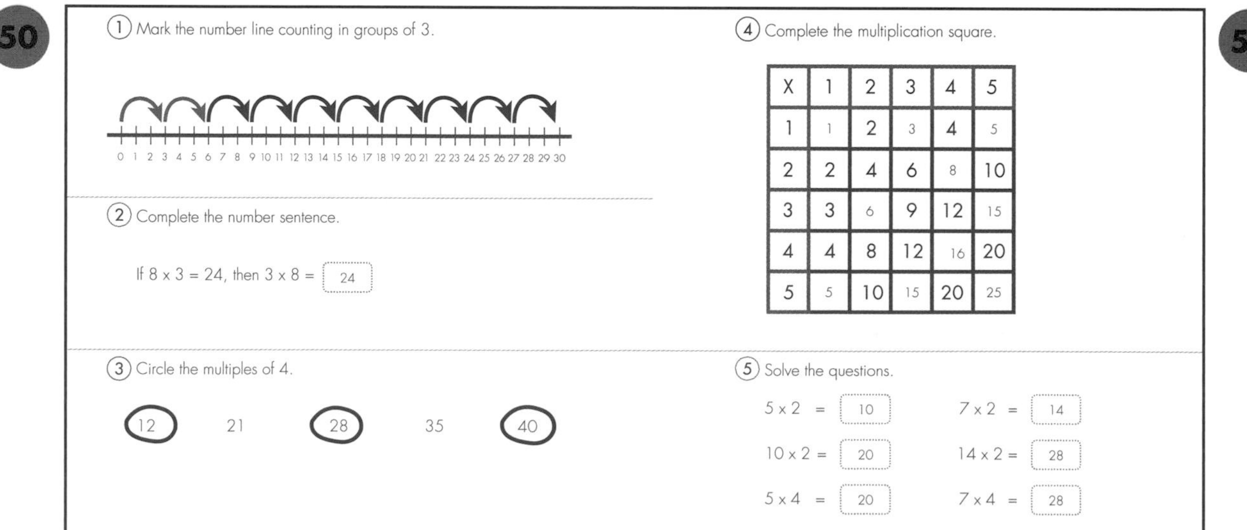

(1) Mark the number line counting in groups of 3.

(2) Complete the number sentence.

If 8 x 3 = 24, then 3 x 8 = 24

(3) Circle the multiples of 4.

12 21 28 35 40

(4) Complete the multiplication square.

X	1	2	3	4	5
1	1	2	3	4	5
2	2	4	6	8	10
3	3	6	9	12	15
4	4	8	12	16	20
5	5	10	15	20	25

(5) Solve the questions.

5 x 2 = 10 7 x 2 = 14

10 x 2 = 20 14 x 2 = 28

5 x 4 = 20 7 x 4 = 28

51

These pages cover further multiplication practice with 3x and 4x tables as well. Encourage your children to chant or sing the times tables they know to get the facts reinforced in their minds. Times table podcasts can be downloaded from the www.dk.com website.

Answers:

52–53 Diagrams
54–55 Shopping

52

	Odd Numbers	Even Numbers
Less than 10	3	8 6
More than 10	21 15 27	14 32

① Add these numbers to the correct square in this Carroll diagram.

6 15 27 32

② In the diagram, which odd number is less than 10?

3

53

Ant
Fish
Owl
Dog
Lion
Table
Bed
Animals
Has four legs

③ On this Venn diagram, which animals have four legs?

Dog, lion

④ On this diagram, which animals do not have four legs?

Ant, fish, owl

⑤ Add a drawing of a chair onto the diagram.

If your child needs some help, discuss with her/him what goes within each box on the Carroll diagram. For the Venn diagram, can your child explain why some of the words are in the overlapping section of the two circles?

54 55

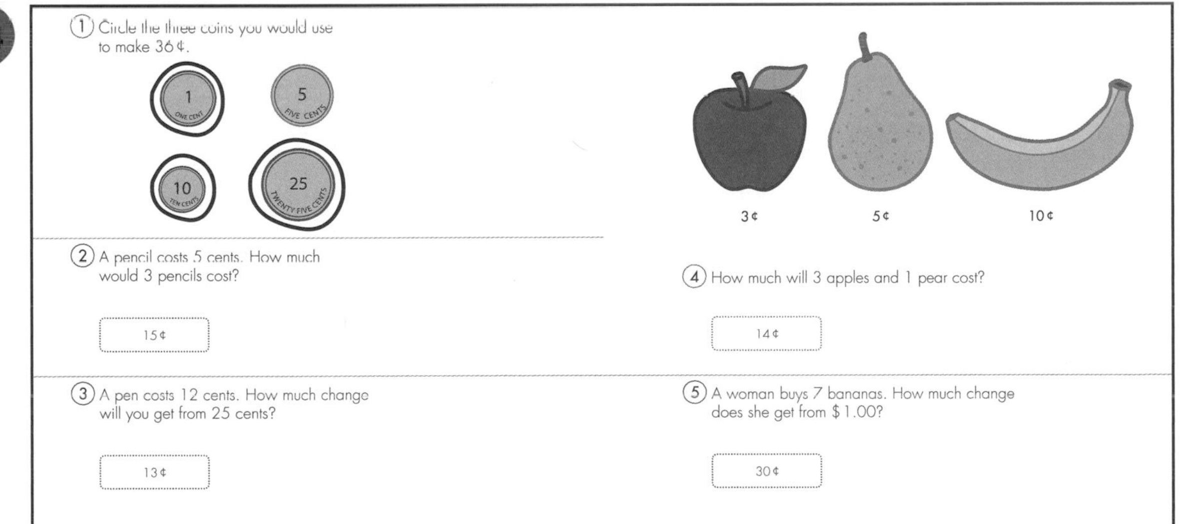

Space has been provided for children to set out their workings or draw to visualize the problem. Remind them to write the unit (¢ or $) for each answer.

There is no "¢" needed if a "$" sign has already been used.

Answers:

56–57 Measuring Speed
58–59 Problem Solving

56

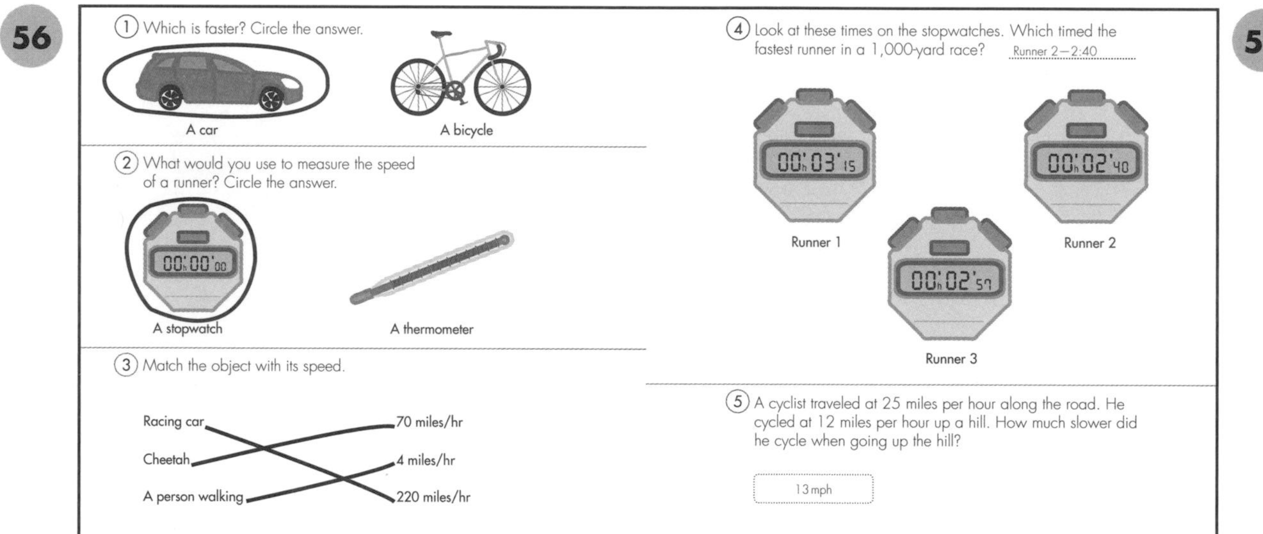

57

Children are introduced to miles per hour as a unit of speed. The questions challenge your child to think about comparing speeds, either based on their knowledge or looking at times on a stopwatch.

If you have a stopwatch, let your child use it to time themselves during an activity such as running from one point to another.

58

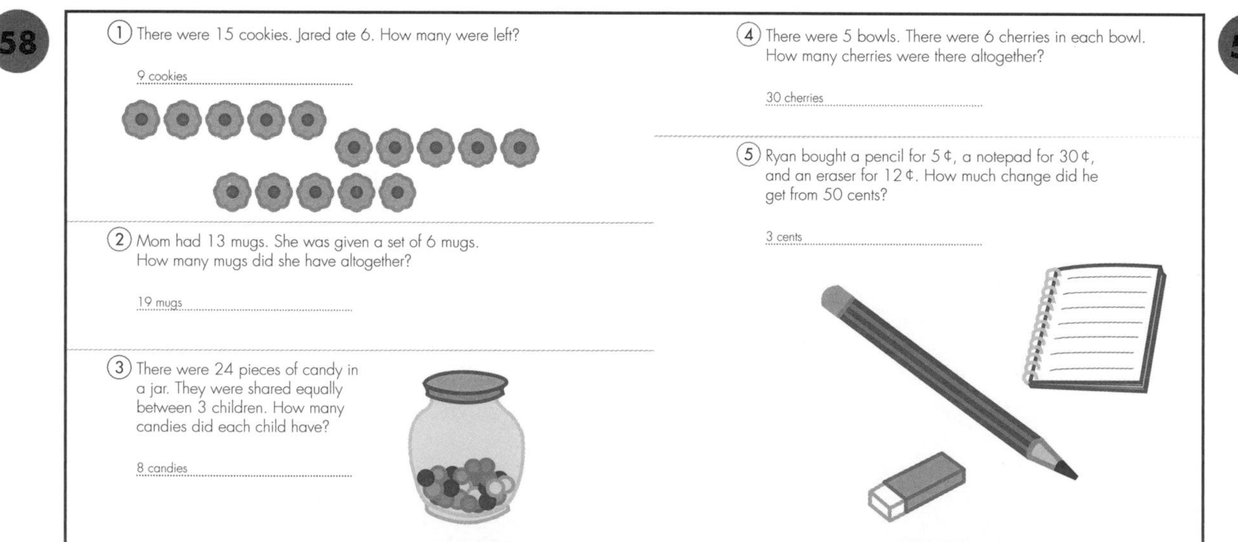

59

For problem solving, children will first have to decide what each question is asking them to do and then work out the best way to calculate the answer.

For example, if they know their 5x table for question 4, it will be quicker to multiply rather than add 6 together five times.

Answers:

60–61 More 3-D Shapes
162–63 Fractions

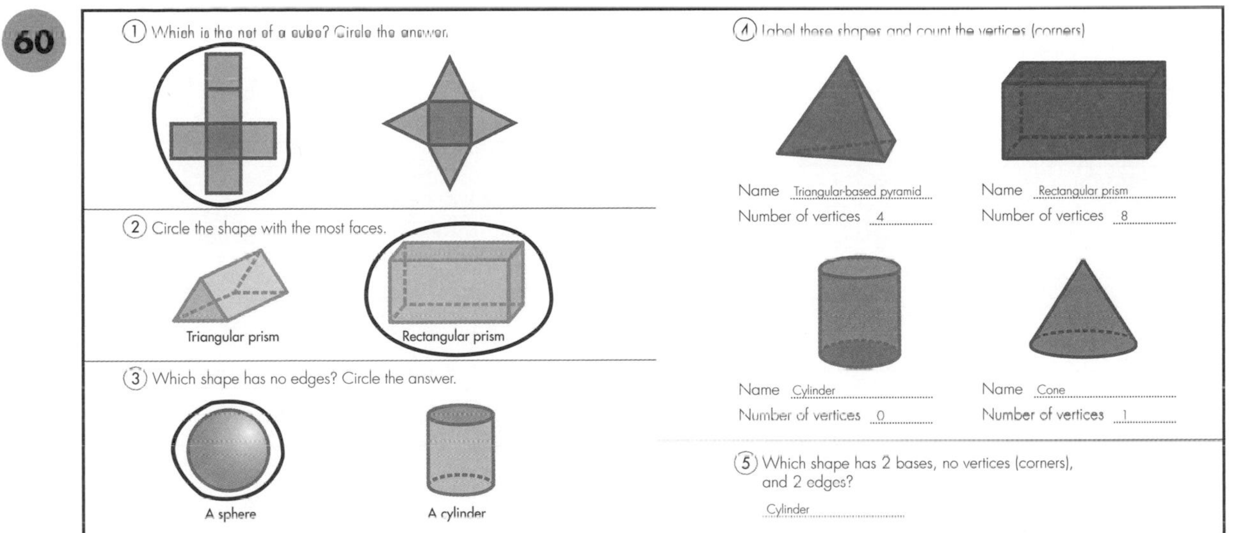

If your child is finding it difficult to count corners or identify faces from the diagrams, let them find real examples of the shapes in the kitchen, bathroom, or among their toys. Ask your child to talk about what makes these 3-D shapes different from one another.

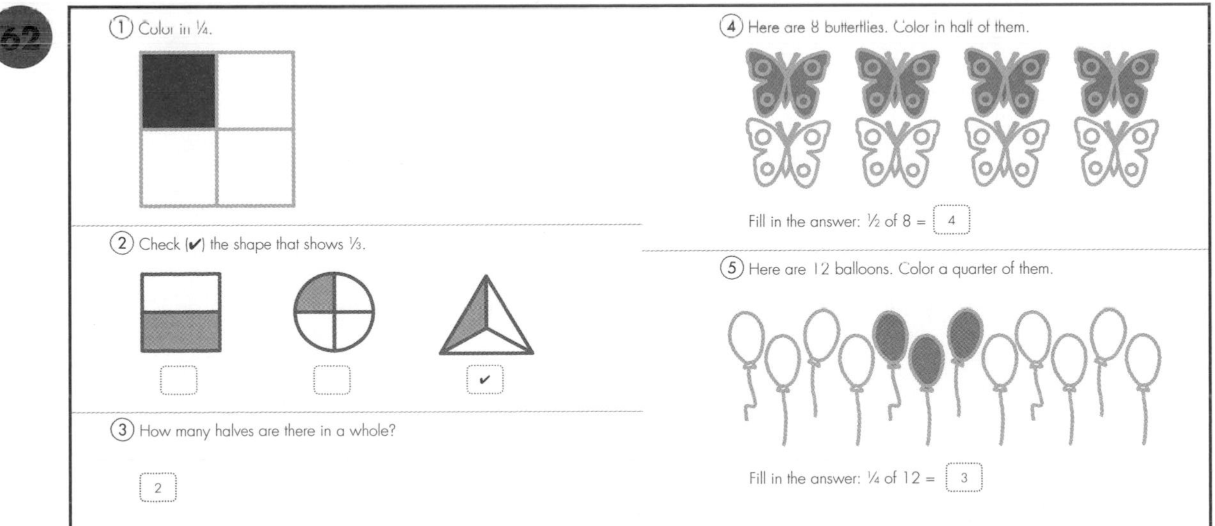

For fractions of numbers and shapes, children should look at the bottom number of the fraction (denominator) to check how many groups the set or shape should be split into. For example, ¼ will need four equal parts. To extend the activity, can your child work out how many balloons would be colored in for two quarters and then three quarters?

Answers:

20–21 Beat the Clock 1
40–41 Beat the Clock 2
64–65 Beat the Clock 3

You may wish to make a photocopy of these pages before your child begins so that she/he can do this exercise a number of times. Although this is against the clock, make sure that children do not feel pressured to rush their answers. It is more important to be accurate. Remind your child that she/he can come back to try and beat the clock at another time.

20													21
	1	9	2	12	3	22	31	87	32	30	33	44	
	4	16	5	3	6	32	34	82	35	61	36	49	
	7	8	8	4	9	11	37	26	38	55	39	10	
	10	1	11	27	12	38	40	77	41	13	42	66	
	13	43	14	18	15	7	43	98	44	73	45	34	
	16	56	17	33	18	14	46	81	47	100	48	25	
	19	21	20	15	21	40	49	60	50	95	51	76	
	22	69	23	80	24	53	52	84	53	37	54	75	
	25	20	26	45	27	51	55	88	56	92	57	57	
	28	19	29	5	30	64	58	48	59	62	60	99	

40													41
	1	9	2	29	3	49	31	3	32	13	33	23	
	4	12	5	42	6	35	34	5	35	35	36	45	
	7	47	8	20	9	60	37	1	38	21	39	71	
	10	38	11	5	12	15	40	11	41	11	42	121	
	13	15	14	3	15	33	43	14	44	74	45	14	
	16	13	17	31	18	32	46	94	47	18	48	88	
	19	12	20	42	21	80	49	15	50	65	51	6	
	22	80	23	40	24	80	52	16	53	7	54	27	
	25	60	26	80	27	80	55	8	56	38	57	7	
	28	100	29	100	30	120	58	7	59	27	60	5	

64													65
	1	4	2	12	3	12	31	2	32	7	33	4	
	4	25	5	12	6	80	34	5	35	1	36	6	
	7	18	8	15	9	14	37	6	38	3	39	3	
	10	21	11	2	12	6	40	4	41	35	42	16	
	13	3	14	2	15	10	43	9	44	100	45	28	
	16	11	17	4	18	8	46	24	47	32	48	27	
	19	1	20	4	21	8	49	80	50	9	51	6	
	22	15	23	7	24	21	52	5	53	8	54	9	
	25	11	26	10	27	20	55	10	56	6	57	9	
	28	20	29	18	30	6	58	12	59	11	60	9	